Running to Win!

A Positive Biblical Approach to Rewards and Inheritance

SECOND EDITION

G. Harry Leafe

About the Author

G. Harry Leafe earned his Bachelor of Biblical Studies degree from College of Biblical Studies, his Master of Theology degree from Dallas Theological Seminary, his Doctor of Ministry degree from Talbot Theological Seminary, and completed post-doctrinal studies in systematic theology at Baptist Bible Seminary.

Library of Congress Cataloging-in Publication Data
Leafe, G. Harry 1940-
   Running to Win!
   112 p.
First Edition:
   ISBN: 0-7375-0027-1
   1. Sanctification. 2. Faith. 3. Salvation
I. Title. II. Title: A Positive Approach to Rewards and inheritance.
Second Edition:
   ISBN: 978-07375-0167-4
   LCCN: 2010901151
   1. Sanctification. 2. Faith. 3. Salvation
I. Title. II. Title: A Positive Approach to Rewards and inheritance.

Table of Contents

To the memory of
John and Barbara McGee

Foreword

"Thy kingdom come!" How many trillions of times has that prayer been made by the children of the Father, but it has probably never been prayed even once with the full realization of what He has in store in the Kingdom for those who endure the pain and follow faithfully to the end of the race. The grand climax of earth's entire history – the age to come – is yet to come. The millennial kingdom – the victory celebration – is going to be shared with that portion of the resurrected/raptured Body of Christ that has paid the price of diligent discipleship.

God has a very definite purpose for the period of time between our justification and our glorification which we call "the race." During the in-between, we are becoming by what we do with what He gave us, what we will be in the climactic kingdom age to come. Today is a day of becoming. Then will be a day of being what we have become. There is continuity – not discontinuity – between how we end the race in this life and how we will reign with Christ (Romans 8:17; 2 Timothy 2:12) in the kingdom climax.

Not until we appear at the Bema (2 Corinthians 5:10) will we receive the final score of the faithful and infallible Judge (1 Corinthians 4:5). And this is a Judge that is really for us. He wants us to receive a "full reward" (2 John v. 8). But He cannot reward that which has not been earned. This is not a gift. It comes from a life of faithful stewardship of our time, talents, and treasure. But the returns from our investment are unparalleled by anything we have seen, heard or imagined.

Dr. Harry Leafe has done for us all an excellent job of not only exercising careful exegetical skill and theological soundness in Scripture, but he has done it with a positive thrust that creates an appetite to dig into the Scripture and examine this tremendous motivational force that, unfortunately, lies dormant in the thought processes of most Christians – even pastors. See you at the Bema – if not before – for no one will be absent.

Earl D. Radmacher, Th.D.
Chancellor
Western Seminary
Portland, Oregon

Preface

I'm quite sure that it could be argued that one of the greatest – if not the greatest – mysteries in life is life itself. People struggle with its meaning, desperately trying to make sense out of all the *happenings* they encounter every day. What about you? Have you ever felt that way? I have.

A number of years ago my closest friend and his wife were senselessly murdered. And although I could acknowledge God's sovereignty over the affairs of man, I still am perplexed by the question, "Why?"

Life regularly brings tough questions before us, questions for which there seems to be no easy, no truly satisfying answers. In general, however, there is a way to understand them.

For years, our family has enjoyed the challenge of working picture puzzles. In our home we have normally kept a puzzle on a small table, to be worked on as anyone had interest. Some have involved thousands of pieces. With several thousand pieces in disarray on the table, you can imagine how overwhelming it can seem! They're of every imaginable shape, and appear as if someone just randomly splattered them with various colors – intentionally without rhyme or reason.

The initial impression is this – and you see how this speaks to the question we are addressing: by themselves alone, the pieces do not seem to have meaning.

Of course, in the case of picture puzzles, there is a way to access the meaning hidden in the separate pieces. Our family quickly learned the secret. All one had to do was to look at the complete picture on the front of the box. Having the entire picture in view provides the assurance that there is indeed meaning to those individual pieces.

Well, you say, this is obvious. But isn't this perhaps limited to picture puzzles? Isn't this because the picture was there to begin with, and then it was cut up into pieces? After all, it isn't really just random pieces. I've discovered that life is very much like a picture puzzle. The analogy is quite appropriate. Let me explain further.

We can feel the sadness for people who have no relationship with Jesus Christ. Not knowing Him is cause enough for sadness, but must we not ask whether they've had the privilege of having God's larger picture to guide them? If indeed they do not possess that picture, there is no way for them to make sense of those separate, confusing pieces of life they can and do see. From the very start, something is missing. Is it any wonder, then, that our society's educators and leaders – psychiatrists, psychologists, professors and others – can offer little if any comfort or hope, let alone direction? For apart from a personal relationship with Christ, they themselves have no idea what the larger, overall picture looks like, and hence have nothing to share with others.

How different it is for all who are trusting in the Lord Jesus Christ! In the Bible they have the complete picture from which to gain a perspective on all of life – a picture clear and beautiful! There for all to read is God's plan for the forgiveness of sin, the gift of eternal life, the way of life abundant, yes, and with fullness of peace and joy!

Theologically, we refer to this overall picture as the sovereign, eternal plan of God. It was formulated, not in time, but in eternity past, with the ultimate goal God's own glory. It is a plan to make Him known as He manifests all of His marvelous attributes in heaven and on earth! Inasmuch as that plan contains everything that will ever come to pass in God's sovereign appointment, it is complete; it sets forth the complete picture. Still, except to the extent that God has chosen to reveal it in His Word, the detail of that plan is unknowable to us. In the revelation of His Word we learn about sweeping things included in His overall purpose for the future, but are not given to know the times and details before they come to pass. As His purposes unfold, we shall be given understanding. This is His promise.

The events of life are like the pieces of a puzzle. God's sovereign plan is like the picture on the box. He has provided enough information about His sovereign plan to give us a picture of life as He intended it and as He shall fulfill it. Little is said in the Bible about the pieces. He leaves it to us – within the means of day-by-day guidance, which He provides – to ponder how the pieces fit into the overall plan.

Sometimes a small piece of the puzzle makes little or no sense; it doesn't appear to fit anywhere at all. Nonetheless we can take it by faith that every piece indeed has its place. Why? Because God designed the picture, formulated the pieces as integral to the whole, and He Himself is working them all together to bring about the completed design.

It is the purpose of this book to help God's people to understand the big picture in order to make sense out of the little pieces that may be impeding spiritual progress. So we ask, what is it that God is doing? Where do we – humanity in its present state, and especially we, believe we are headed? Bringing it down to our personal lives, what is His purpose for me, for you? How do the decisions you and I make fit into His plan – or do they? What relationship do they have to our inheritance and rewards in Christ? These are but a few of the important questions addressed in this book.

It is the author's desire that for all those who read these pages, this message will become for them a clear and certain aid in meeting their quest to know Him, and to be properly and assuredly oriented to His glorious plan.

G. Harry Leafe
Houston, Texas

1

Discovering the True Meaning of Life

In the late 1950s there was a popular television program called *This Is Your Life*. The main idea of the program was to select an individual as the focal point, and then to bring in people from his or her past who upon their entrance were for awhile out of the individual's line of vision. They began to speak about something from their past relationship, anticipating that the subject person would recognize them. The various people from the past were brought on in an order intended to convey an overview of the subject's life.

I remember first watching this program as a teenager, wondering what my life would look like over time if I were the subject, that is, what my life would look like if represented by a time line? One way would be to draw a line on a piece of paper, set it off in five-year segments, and then begin to pinpoint specific events that highlight each segment. When finished I would have a visual representation of the highlighted continuum of my life to present.

The initial question is this: Of what does my life consist? If someone were to evaluate it, upon what basis would they do so? These are important questions, particularly in light of Paul's statement in 2 Corinthians 5:10, "For we must all appear before the judgment seat of Christ, so that each one may be paid back according to what he has done while in the body, whether good or evil."

In order to understand the basis upon which God will judge our lives, we need to know the sense in which the word *life* is a biblical term standing for *soul*. In as much as this is the meaning, we must then ask, as we advance further, How is the term *soul* defined?

The Meaning of Soul

As recorded in Matthew 16:24, our Lord told his disciples that to follow him would be costly. Here is how he put it: *"Then Jesus said to his disciples, 'If anyone wants to become my follower, he must deny himself, take up his cross, and follow me.'"* The statement is clearly in the context of committed discipleship. Earlier in his ministry Jesus had explained to Nicodemus the way of salvation. It was by faith in him alone. As we shall note in our next segment, salvation from sin was not explained in terms of denying one's self, or in taking up one's cross, but rather in terms of simple faith in Christ. Consider John 3:16, "For this is the way God loved the world: he gave his one and only Son, so that everyone who believes in him will not perish but have eternal life." The Lord continued on to then explain about the cost of following him.

The reason the issue is so critical is stated in Matthew 16:25, "For whoever wants to save his life will lose it, but whoever loses his life on account of me will find it." From this statement it should be clear that Jesus is talking about the motivation of one's heart, and what issues from such motivation. In other words, it puts forth a contrast between a person trying to please himself and a person trying to please Christ.

In both instances where the word *life* appears in verse 25, it is a translation of the Greek term *psuchē* (soul). In the progression of thought, this ties into the next verse, "For what does it benefit a person if he gains the whole world but forfeits his life? Or what can a person give in exchange for his life?"

2

When we consider a person's life, as the term is used in this context, it will be helpful to determine a more precise meaning. Of just what does one's life consist? And in what sense can one exchange it for something? And this something for which it may be exchanged – what does it have to do with the event mentioned by Paul, "For we must all appear before the judgment seat of Christ"?

Notice Jesus' complementing statement in verse 27, "For the Son of Man will come with his angels in the glory of his Father, and then he will reward each person according to what he has done."

The term "reward" (Gr. *apodidōmi*) means "to render or give back what is due." The Greek-English Lexicon of Arndt and Gingrich, as well as that of Liddell and Scott, agree as to the meaning of the term – that whatever is due may relate to either good or bad. If a person is to receive something from the Lord that is *due* him, whether good or bad, certainly this does not concern salvation from sin (cf. Rom. 4:1-5), but rather, to something that indeed can be earned. So just what does Paul have in mind?

Paul's words, both in 2 Cor. 5:10 and Eph. 6:8 carry the same truth. In the phrase, "... that each one may be paid back for what he has done while in the body" (the Corinthian passage), he uses the Greek word *komizō* (paid back), the same as in the Ephesian passage, "you know that each person, whether slave or free, if he does something good, will be rewarded *(komizō)* by the Lord."

The concept of receiving a wage due one is even stronger with *komizō* than with *apodidōmi*! Certainly, "to get for one's self by earning" is not related to salvation from sin, since we are told that "For *by grace* you are saved through faith, and this is not from yourselves, *it is the gift of God, it is not for works, so that no one can boast*" (Eph. 2:8-9, italics mine).

Whatever comprises one's life becomes the basis of the wage due or reward earned. We've already observed that our works play a part in the transaction. But the term "works" itself seems to include the total product of one's life. Helpfully, the term can be expanded to include other components of a specific nature. For example, our Lord said, "I tell you that on the day of judgment, people will give an account for every worthless word they speak." (Matt. 12:36). Further, the Bible speaks to the matter of our thinking or reasoning processes when it says, "So then, do not judge anything before the time. Wait until the Lord comes. He will bring to light the hidden things of darkness and reveal *the motives of hearts*. Then each will receive recognition from God" (1 Cor. 4:5, italics mine).

Before giving a final definition to the term "life" as our Lord used it in Matthew 16 and elsewhere, it is important to remember that words are often used in different ways. Recall that in the verses we have discussed, the term life is actually a translation of the Greek term for soul. And the Greek term soul can be used in several ways.

For example, simply looking at how human beings are constituted, we conclude that they are basically two-part beings. We are both material and non-material. To describe various functions of our non-material being, various words are used: spirit, mind, heart, conscience, feelings, etc. Very often the term soul is used in this same way. All of these terms are used to describe the various functions of our non-material self.

Sometimes, however, a term can be used to describe the whole of something, and it is in this sense that the term soul is used in Matthew 16; it describes the whole of a person's life. When used in this way, it can be defined as *the total temporal expression of human life*. It is what we shall refer to as "soul-life."

4

Having previously identified those aspects of a person's life that are subject to God's judgment, we are now able to see that a person's life (soul-life) has three essential components: thoughts, words and actions. Together, the sum of these make up our lives as lived during our time upon earth. It is obvious that some of our thoughts are proper, some are not. The same is true of words and actions.

Keep in mind that what we are endeavoring to present in these pages is the big picture of God's program for training His children. We are not discussing the lives of unbelievers, but believers. Theologically speaking, it is process of *sanctification* – the process that takes us from being children to being adults in God's family.

With Eternity's Values in Mind?

People have different ideas about that of which life consists. Some think it is an abundance of material possessions, for to them, this means importance, security, often a sense of "I've got the resources; I can handle anything!" Others see education and its attendant honors as the essence of life. Still others think relationships with other people provide the key to life abundant. It may well be that many of these same people give some place, however superficially, to God. But is it the proper place? Should He not be central to their lives?

The real problem is one of priority, God's imperative place which Jesus taught His disciples. To follow Him would mean putting Him first. In whatever we think, say, or do, to put Him first has more than temporal value. It has eternal value. Conversely, the thinking, saying or doing that puts ourselves first has temporal value only, not eternal value.

Paul set forth this principle in his admonition to salves in Ephesians 6. They were to serve their masters "… in

5

the sincerity of your heart as to Christ, not like those who do their work only when someone is watching – as people pleasers – but as slaves of Christ doing the will of God from the heart" (vv. 5-6).

Having a desire to gratify *self* comes quite naturally, as most of us would grant. We are sinners, and as such are self-serving. Although the tendency will always remain, growing in Christ will make us less so. Paul warned the Philippians about this: "In stead of being motivated by selfish ambition or vanity, each of you should, in humility, be moved to treat one another as more important than yourself. Each of you should be concerned not only about your own interests, but about the interests of others as well" (2:3-4).

Seeking to *save one's life* as Jesus put it is to be temporally oriented. Losing one's life for Christ's sake is to be oriented to eternity. This, as we shall see, lends significance to Jesus' question, "What will a man give in exchange for his soul?"

Keeping in mind that "life" stands for "soul-life," how might this truth be illustrated? Is there a way to quantify our soul-life? Let's assign it a certain time-value, maybe 70 years. And let's give it a dollar value, perhaps $1,440,000 (an annual income of $36,000 for 40 years). On this scale of values, how much of one's money would be invested in people, places and things that have only temporal value – the consequence of such investment having no more than temporal worth? In other words, what portion of one's investment ought to relate to life in earthly time, how much to life in eternity? Have you considered life in terms of this scale of values? Let's return to Jesus' concept of saving or losing one's life.

When Our Soul Shall Be Required of Us

We are daily told by well-meaning people that we have lots of unmet needs that rightfully are to be taken care of. The suggestion is that unless and until these personal needs are met, we cannot adequately minister to those around us. We are to love ourselves, feel good about ourselves, grow in self-esteem and the sense of self-worth. *Then* we can reach beyond ourselves to serve others. *Then* we can extend our love to other people.

The Bible, however, never speaks in these terms. First, we are never told to love ourselves. Assumably, we do this quite naturally (cf. Eph. 5:29; Matt. 22:39). Further, we are never told to be concerned about personal needs. On the contrary, Jesus taught His disciples that when they followed that philosophy of life – putting self first – they were actually doing what unbelievers were, by nature, disposed to do (cf. Matt. 6:32). As followers of Him, they (and we) are to "above all pursue his kingdom and righteousness, and all these things will be given to you as well" (Matt. 6:33).

God gave a similar answer to Paul who prayed for deliverance from a personal affliction. In this case, God's reply to his perceived need was, "My grace is enough for you, for my power is made perfect in weakness" (2 Cor. 12:9).

Sometimes He chooses to deliver us, sometimes not. Ultimately, it is His sovereign will that matters. Ours is to seek first His kingdom and righteousness, and then as He sees fit, He appoints for us that which will meet our true needs.

Doesn't this really strike at the heart of the problem? Are we going to occupy ourselves with those things that are merely temporal, or are we going to pursue that which is eternal?

Note how the Lord Jesus speaks to this. After telling His disciples not to be concerned about themselves, but rather, about pleasing and serving God, He related the blessedness of the Father's concern, how He will take care of them.

The world cannot see it this way, for to suggest that one not be concerned for himself does not make sense. Who, if not ourselves, will? But, contrary to the world's reasoning, God's plan for His children is the divinely designated way to true happiness and fulfillment in this life. Abundant living is truly there for us, but only as it is found in a personal, living relationship with the Lord Jesus Christ (cf. Jn. 10:10).

To further clarify His point, Jesus told a story (Lk. 12:13-21). The subject of the story is a businessman who, at that time, had great wealth. Moreover, his business continued to prosper. What will he do with so much? Self-centered in his thinking, his words and actions consistently focused in the same direction. His reasoning was as follows: "I will do this: I will tear down my barns and build bigger ones, and there I will store all my grain and my goods. And I will say to myself, 'you have many goods stored up for many years; relax, eat, drink, celebrate!'" (vv.18-19).

Sound reasonable? Take a look at God's response: "You fool! This very night your life will be demanded back from you, but who will get what you have prepared for yourself?" (v.20). Do you identify the basic problem? He had invested his life in that which had only temporal value, only transient worth. And when he died, all he had acquired was gone!

Apply this to those who follow Him, who seek to do His bidding. They, too, must not overlook the lesson: "So it is with the one who stores up riches *for himself*, and is not rich toward God" (v.21, italics mine). A person can be rich in the world's eyes, yet not rich toward God. Or he can be rich toward God, although not rich in the world's value system. This is what Jesus meant by saving or losing our lives.

Saved and Being Saved

In the Holy Land, the town of Caesarea Philippi is situated on the southern slopes of Mount Hermon, located north of the Sea of Galilee. When the Greeks came into the area following the conquest of Alexander the Great, they established a shrine for one of their gods, Pan. These Greeks believed that Hades was located beneath the mountain area where the shrine to Pan was established. And inasmuch as the easternmost source of the Jordan River is found at this same location, flowing out from there, they also believed it to be the source of life. Herein is an interesting connection. We can believe that Jesus brought the disciples to this spot for a very important reason!

It was near this pagan site that the Lord Jesus asked His disciples the penetrating question, "Who do people say that the Son of Man is?" (Matt. 16:13). Their reply accurately reflected what the people generally considered to be the case: "Some say John the Baptist, others Elijah, and others Jeremiah or one of the prophets" (v. 14).

Standing in the midst of what represented fallen mankind's understanding of the essence of life, He was now going to take them to the next step in their understanding of the plan of God and the real meaning of life. To do this, He must first show them their own mistaken views.

Jesus directed the questions straight to them: "But who do you say that I am?" Expectedly, Simon Peter acted as spokesman for the group, "You are the Christ, the Son of the living God" (v. 16).

We can make two important observations: First, the disciples had not come to their understanding about Christ on their own. Jesus affirmed this, "… flesh and blood did not reveal this to you, but my Father in heaven!" (v. 17). Second, it is upon Himself (as stated in Peter's confession) "… I will build My church, and the gates of Hades will not overpower it" (v. 18). Peter was a rock, but Jesus Himself was the true foundation upon which the church was to be built, not Peter.

The disciples are being brought along in their understanding of life from God's point of view. From the context, we learn that man's understanding, quite different from God's, is built upon a system we call *Humanism*. And whether in our Lord's day or our own, *Humanism* represents mankind's self-devised search for life.

As they journeyed from Caesarea Philippi, the Lord continued to instruct them about Himself and their relationship to Him. He continued to build new meaning into the term *life*: "… whoever wants to save his life will lose it, but whoever loses his life for my sake will find it" (Matt. 16:25).

Their journey ultimately brought them to Jerusalem, where they would celebrate the Feast of Booths. It was an important occasion, particularly, as it turned out, for the disciples. For on the last day of the feast, a startling thing happened. Jesus stood up in the midst of the great crowd of people and made a loud proclamation. John records the event in this way: "On the last day of the feast, the greatest day, Jesus stood up and shouted out, 'If anyone is thirsty, let him come to me, and let the one who believes in me drink. Just as the Scripture says, *From within him will flow rivers of living water*'" (Jn. 7:37-38).

In Jesus' announcement, the two approaches to life are finally sorted out. What man desperately and falsely

12

seeks at the waters of Humanism is declared to reside truly in Jesus Christ and is available to all those who place their faith in Him. We now know something more of what life consists.

Praise For A Living Hope

Before the advent of the Holy Spirit and the beginning experiences of New Covenant blessings, Peter, like the other disciples, had a difficult time trying to put two and two together spiritually. Jesus explained this difficulty to Peter when He said, "you do not understand what I am doing now, but you will understand after these things" (Jn. 13:7). This inability had existed throughout the whole three and a half years that he and the others had spent with the Lord. But things were to be different in the future. That same evening, Jesus said to all of them, "But, when he, the Spirit of truth, comes, he will guide you into all truth. For he will not speak on his own authority, but will speak whatever he hears, and will tell you what is to come. He will glorify me, because he will receive from me what is mine and will tell it to you" (Jn. 16:13-14).

By the time he wrote his first epistle, Peter had put it all together. He had come to understand the connection between soul-life, rivers of living water, and faith in Christ. Moreover, he had come to understand that soul-life has a relationship to the events of time, although always with a view to eternity. As he addresses the subject, he begins where Jesus began with him: God's saving grace and the hope (confidence) that it brings to those who believe in Christ.

Listen to Peter: "Blessed be the God and Father of our Lord Jesus Christ! By his great mercy *he gave us new birth* into a living hope through the resurrection of Jesus Christ from the dead" (1 Pet. 1:3, italics mine). Salvation is the work of God. Man's inability to respond to the re-

13

velation of God (cf. Rom. 3:9-18; 8:5-8) necessitates a work of God's grace in the heart if any are to be saved. At the moment of salvation, the truth of the Gospel of Christ is revealed, and through the Holy Spirit, faith to believe is granted. Thus, through this transaction, a person is *given new birth into a living hope*.

We need to distinguish Peter's view of "hope" from that of the world. Peter does not imply that hope has some degree of uncertainty. From the biblical perspective, hope expresses certainty – the confidence of hope engendered by the Holy Spirit and grounded upon God's sure Word. Our Sovereign, all-powerful God will do as He has decreed!

Our salvation from the penalty of sin and salvation's related hope is with a view to an inheritance that is to be revealed in the future. Moreover, we read that it is an inheritance "imperishable, undefiled, and unfading. It is reserved in heaven for you" (1 Pet. 1:4). It is an inheritance for us who believe in Christ. And the question is not whether we will *get there* to receive it, but rather, *how much* of it will we receive. Receiving a full inheritance is conditional, as we shall see in the ongoing chapters.

Here is a fundamental point that must not be underestimated. Once we have been saved from the penalty of sin through faith in Christ, it is not possible for us to be lost again. Why? Because we are not saved on the basis of our own goodness or works, but by the redemptive provision of God's unmerited grace. Even the faith to believe is not generated on our own, but is a gift of God (cf. Eph. 2:8-9; Phil. 1:28). This being so, what is it that keeps me saved? My goodness as a believer? My Christian works? No! The power of God and that alone! Salvation is not preserved by good works!

Now look carefully at Peter's word in verse 5: "... who by God's power are protected through faith... ." The word "protected" is a translation of the Greek *phroureō*. There are some important things about the way this word is used here. First, it is a verb expressed in the present tense; it concerns something continuing on in the present time. Use of the passive voice indicates that it is something being done *to* us. Of equal importance, *phroureō* uniquely means "to keep in a state of security." That aspect is vital!

What is underscored is that we who are believers in Christ are being kept in a state of secured salvation by the power of God, and all this is with a view to an inheritance still future. No wonder Peter exclaims, "This brings you great joy" (v. 6). What a hope is ours! What security is ours!

Recall once more that Peter had come to understand that soul-life has a connection with events in time, Midway in verse 6, he begins to explain that connection. Note the qualifying phrase attached to, "This brings you great joy." While rejoicing in the inheritance awaiting us in heaven, we meet Peter's "although you may have to suffer for a short time in various trials." The reality is that we are to expect trials as a necessary element in Christian living, a testing by trials, as stated in verse 7, and this has to do with "the proven character of your faith." What, then, is the connection?

Proof of Faith

The trials Peter has in mind are designed by our heavenly Father to prove the character of our faith (not destroy it!). To be sure, trials also demonstrate lack of faith. But the issue here is the *proven character* (Gr. *dokimion*) of our faith, said to be "more valuable than gold – gold that is tested by fire, even though it is passing away – ."

15

The clear implication is that gold, in this analogy, has only temporary value, while the *proven character* of faith has eternal value. This is further expressed in the outcome – such proven faith results in "praise and glory and honor when Jesus Christ is revealed."

Another important point needs to be made with regard to the *proven character* of our faith. We will get into this more later, but Peter uses *proven character* of faith to indicate what the Bible also calls *good works*. Our evaluations and responses to the concerns of life will issue either from faith in the provisions of God's grace, or in our own self-sufficiency. In either case, a work is produced. If the work issues from our faith in God, it is a *good work* (cf. Rom. 14:23b; Eph. 2:10). It reveals the *proven character* of our faith. All our works, good and bad, will be "tested by fire" at the judgment seat of Christ (cf. 1 Cor. 3:10-15). The judgment by fire is to test the *quality* of our works (v. 13). *Good works* (*proven* faith) become the basis for reward (v. 14). This is precisely what Peter has in mind when he says that the character of our faith having been proven (in the analogy of gold "tested by fire"), will result in "praise and glory and honor" (terms related to rewards). And it will happen "when Jesus Christ is revealed." To put it another way, the character of our faith is proven in time, but that proof is demonstrated and rewarded in the future, at the judgment seat of Christ.

Can we believe in and actually serve someone we've never seen? That, you may say, takes real faith! Yes, it does, and that's exactly what Peter insists is our present condition. Notice how he frames it in verse 8: "You have not seen him, but you love him. You do not see him now but you believe in him, and so you rejoice with an indescribable and glorious joy"

Clearly, then, the trials we experience in life are designed to test our faith, and of necessity, the testing in-

16

volves our thoughts, words and actions. This being the case, will we then evaluate our circumstances on the basis of God's Word – a biblical worldview – or on some other basis, whatever that might be? Will the intent of our words be to minister and to build up those around us? Will the purpose of our actions be to demonstrate our faith in Christ? If these responses issue from faith in God and His Word, then they become what Peter calls the *proven character* of our faith. And that proven faith will be demonstrated and rewarded "when Jesus Christ is revealed," an event of great importance, and as we shall see later, one that plays a vital role in the development of this book.

The Salvation of Your Soul

Recall from Chapter 1 the discussion about our ability to save our soul-life. We learned that the issue is one of *sanctification*, not of salvation from the penalty of sin. We also learned that our soul-life consists of our thoughts, words and actions. Some of these issue from faith, others do not. Those of faith have eternal value, while the others have only temporal significance. Recall, too, that our Lord stated, "For whoever wants to save his life will lose it, but whoever loses his life for my sake will save it" (Luke 9:24).

The term *save* (Gr. *sōzō*) means "to rescue, liberate, preserve, deliver." The question is this: What did our Lord mean when He used this term? He taught us that in some manner, we can exchange the temporal experiences of human life for that which is eternal: "Accumulate for yourselves treasures in heaven" (Matt. 6:20); "What does it benefit a person if he gains the whole world and forfeits his life? Or what can a person give in exchange for his life?" (Matt. 16:26). And in so doing, we actually *save* our soul-life from time to eternity (cf. Lk. 12:20-21). Clearly, Jesus meant *to deliver* our soul-life, which also happens to be the primary meaning of the term in the New Testament.

But what can Peter add from *his* understanding of what Jesus taught about this matter? How does *this* salvation work itself out in life? In the passage before us, notice how he has developed a connection between "an inheritance" (v. 4), "a salvation" (v. 5), and the "praise and glory and honor" (v. 7) – all of which are associated with "the revelation of Jesus Christ" (v. 7). The "inheritance" is what awaits us in heaven. "Praise and glory and honor" reflects the reception of our portion of that inheritance. But what about "a salvation?"

It is difficult for grace-oriented believers to think in terms of earning anything from God. Certainly, salvation from the penalty of sin is a free gift of God's grace. However, Peter now tells us that we attain (Gr. *komizō*) as the goal of our faith "the salvation of our souls" (v. 9). Clearly, the salvation of verse 5 is the same as verse 9, "a salvation ready to be revealed in the last time." Recall from Chapter 1 that *komizō* means "to receive something that is due, or to get for oneself by earning."

The point is clear. Our share in the inheritance is determined by that portion of our soul-life that is saved or delivered into eternity. And *that* salvation is demonstrated by our good works or, as Peter put it, the *proven character* of faith. We receive inheritance on the basis of our *demonstrated* faith (good works). And that is what "salvation of the soul" is all about!

18

3

The Character of Your Faith

Recently I was watching the evening news on television, and during the first commercial break, a beautiful woman appeared and exclaimed, "I've had it with reality! I want illusion!" What did she mean? It was a come-on.

Although she was talking about her appearance and how a certain brand of cosmetics could make her look like something she was not, I was suddenly struck by the philosophy of life represented by her statement (not hers, of course, but put in her mouth by the cosmetic company's ad people). People *do* live in a world of illusion, whether they are aware of it or not. People *do* mask the reality of their lives so that others will see something other than what is really there. Every one of us tends to live behind a façade of our own devising. All too often, our lives betray an altogether, unreal quality, a certain inauthenticity.

What others see in us – is this really what's there? What are we leading others to believe we are? In reality, are the true characteristics of our lives the fruit of the Spirit, or are we merely mastering the technique of pretense – *emulating* Christlikeness in outward behavior only, without the conforming, inner work of the Spirit? Are we more concerned that people *think* we are spiritual, despite our knowing we are not?

What about you? Has your life become a life of illusion? Is or is not your life an authentic enactment of your faith – really, now? What answer fits you best?

Faith That Works

In 1 Pet. 1:7, the Apostle wrote, "the proven character of your faith, which is more valuable than gold – gold that is tested by fire, even though it is passing away – and will bring praise and glory and honor when Jesus Christ is revealed." Notice once again that it is the *proven character* of our faith that is more precious than gold. Why? Because it will result in "praise and honor and glory" at the revelation of Jesus Christ. Proven faith, as we have seen, is an expression for what the Bible calls good works, works which become the basis of our share in the inheritance in Christ.

The words "Such trials" which begin the verse take us back to the statement of verse 6, "... although you may have to suffer for a short time in various trials." Here is an interesting connection. Our faith is proven in the context of life's normal activities and circumstances. Within the activities and circumstances, the trials or tests of our faith appear. To repeat an earlier statement, how we evaluate and respond to the concerns of life will either issue from faith in the provisions of God's grace, or from faith in our own sufficiency. What results – our thoughts, words and actions – will betray the real intent of our heart, and thus, the *character* of our faith.

The Value of Proven Faith

It was well known to Peter that a clear relationship exists between how we handle the tests of our faith and our inheritance in Christ. A proper faith-response proves the character of our faith, and our proven faith results in reward and inheritance – the salvation of our soul. But as clearly as Peter has stated these truths, it does not present the total picture.

James, the writer of the epistle that bears his name, himself the half-brother of our Lord, was also aware of the relationship between trials and faith and how proper faith responses are a part of the development process that matures and completes the child of God and prepares him for his inheritance.

Even though he did not come to believe in his elder brother as Messiah until after Jesus had been raised from the dead, James had been exposed to what He had taught on many occasions (cf. Matt. 12:46-50; 13:55, 56; Jn. 2:12; 7:3, 5). Can it be assumed, then, that James understood about soul-life and the concept of the salvation of the soul as Peter had? Let's take a look.

A close look at his epistle will reveal that James uses the term "save" (Gr. *sōzō*) five times. But not once does he use it in a context dealing with salvation from the penalty of sin. In fact, there is not even a hint that there may be an unbeliever in his audience. Nineteen times he refers to his readers as brethren. The book is really a handbook on Christian living.

Let's look at two of his usages of the term save. The first is in 1:21, where he urges his readers to "welcome the message implanted within you, which is able to *save your souls*" (italics mine). Notice the connection that he makes between salvation of the soul and obedience to the Word as he continues, "But be sure you live out the message and do not merely listen to it and so deceive yourselves" (v. 22). To James, a life of faith is a life lived in obedience to the Word of God. It is a life that issues in a product – proven faith.

"My brothers and sisters, do not show prejudice if you possess faith in our glorious Lord Jesus Christ," James says (2:1). The NET Bible notes a more strict translation: "Do not have faith with personal prejudice." As believers in Christ, we all have faith. It was a gift to us at the moment of our regeneration by the Spirit of God. But just having it is not an end in itself. It must be exercised to have value, but exercised appropriately within the normal circumstances of life. James offers a good example in the next verses when he relates the exercise of our faith to the way we tend to judge people.

Loving our neighbor as ourselves means that we treat all people equitably. Because one has wealth and prestige as judged by our culture does not give the right to neglect one who is less fortunate. In fact, when any of us does so, it indicates we are not living in faithful obedience to God's Word, which tells us to love our neighbor as ourselves!

This commandment, to love our neighbor as ourselves, is the second of the two great commandments as delineated by our Lord, the first being to love God with all our heart, soul and mind. These two commandments comprise what James variously calls "The Perfect Law" (1:25); "The Law of Liberty" (1:25); and "The Royal Law (2:8). They touch every aspect and moment of life and teach us that our lives should be lived as those who will be judged by them (2:12).

Having developed this progression of obedient faith – a faithful obedience to God's Word, fleshed out in the circumstances of life within the parameters of the Royal Law – a vitally important question is asked, "What good is it, my brothers and sisters, if someone claims to have faith but does not have works? Can this kind of faith save him?" The answer demanded by the text is a firm *no*. But "save" in what sense? Recall that James has already said that a reception of the "implanted word" ultimately issues in the salvation of the soul. By reception, James means more than just hearing it or believing it to be true. He means receiving it with the thought of living in faithful obedience to it, the results of which are works of faith.

The context is one of judgment. In the future, the Believer will not face judgment for sin – Christ died for our sins. Therefore, the judgment before us must be what Paul calls "the judgment seat of Christ" (2 Cor. 5:10). And it is at the judgment seat of Christ that our works of faith will be rewarded. They actually become the basis of our portion of the inheritance in Christ (we will develop this in a later chapter). Since our works of faith represent our soul-life (we developed this in the first two chapters), we are, by our obedient responses, saving our souls.

Suppose, as James is doing, that a person says he lives by faith. How are we to know that what he is saying is actually true? Can faith alone save (deliver) his soul (soul-life)? It is important to repeat that James is not talking about salvation from the penalty of sin. Rather, he is talking about the same thing Peter talked about when he said that our share in the inheritance is determined by that portion of our soul-life that is saved or delivered into eternity. And *that* salvation is demonstrated by our good works or *proven* faith. We receive inheritance on the basis of our *demonstrated* faith (good works). And that is what "salvation of the soul" is all about! Just having faith without obedient responses through works is not enough.

Every believer in Christ has faith, but it is what is produced by that faith that gives it its reality and value. There is no better example than that of Abraham offering his son, Isaac, as a sacrifice (2:21-24). Abraham had faith. God had earlier proclaimed him righteous on the basis of it – apart from any works whatsoever (Gen. 15:6; Rom. 4:1-25). Now, many years later, in the providence of God, he is being placed in a situation where his faith is to be "proven."

23

Abraham's son, Isaac, was the individual through whom God would confirm the covenant. He was the only son of promise. What would Abraham do? How would he reason? Would his evaluation of himself and his circumstances issue from faith in the revelation of God? Would his thoughts, words and actions *prove* the *character* of his faith?

The writer of Hebrews provides some important insight into this event: "By faith Abraham, when he was tested, offered up Isaac. He had received the promises, yet he was ready to offer up his only son. God had told him, *'Through Isaac descendants will carry on your name,'* and he reasoned that God could even raise him from the dead" (11:17-19). Please note that Abraham thought "biblically." His actions were based on faith in his "biblical reasonings." In a word, his works of faith proved the character of his faith. He was justified (in the sense of being vindicated) before men – not before God. Remember, that had occurred earlier.

Therefore, James arrives at the conclusion: "For just as the body without the spirit is dead, so also faith without works is dead" (v. 26). That is, such faith, in terms of the salvation of the soul, is as useless as a dead body!

Be Prepared For The Pop Quizzes!

When I was a student at Dallas Seminary, my Greek professor was famous for his daily "pop quizzes." Not to have a pop quiz was a rare exception! It kept you on your toes. And we never knew what form they would take. One day, I might have been asked to write out vocabulary words. On another, I might have been called upon to recite the Greek alphabet. And still on another, I might have been invited to the chalkboard to write out and diagram a sentence from the Greek New Testament. The important point was this: Be prepared. It was not a question of "if" a quiz was coming, only "when!"

James actually begins his epistle with this same thought: "Consider it nothing but joy when you fall into all sorts of trials" (1:2). With James, the matter of trials or tests of faith (what I like to call "pop quizzes") was not a matter of "if" either, only "when."

But why are we to consider it nothing but joy?" What is the basis for such a response? It is our knowledge of the relationship between faith, tests of faith, maturity, and our inheritance in Christ. "Because you know," he says, "that the testing of your faith produces endurance. And let endurance have its perfect effect, so that you may be perfect and complete, not deficient in anything" (vv. 3-4).

It should be very obvious by this time that the tests of our faith come in the normal activities and circumstances of life. In that regard, we can say that everything we face in life is a test of faith. Why? Because we are called upon to evaluate the basis of it. Will these words, then, edify and minister grace to the hearers? Or we may be called upon to perform some action. Will it reflect love for God and/or our neighbor? In other words, will we make a faith-response? Will our thoughts, words and actions prove the godly character of our faith?

It is in a sense unfortunate that almost every English translation reads "the testing of your faith" in verse 3. There is no verb or participle in the Greek text. And it is the same exact phrase that appears in 1 Pet. 1:7, which is consistently translated as "the proven character of your faith." Only in the translation, *Today's English Version*, have I been able to locate a rendering of verse 3 that captures James' meaning: "For you know that when your faith succeeds in facing such trials, the result is the ability to endure."

The point to be emphasized is this. It is not the trials that result in endurance. It is not gritting one's teeth and hanging in there through the difficulties of life. It is, like a math test, working the problems successfully – passing the test, not just taking it!

Proven faith, according to James, results in a product – steadfast endurance (Gr. *hupomonē*). The term means "mental toughness, stick-to-it-iveness." It is a character quality without which we are unable to successfully run "the race of life" (cf. Heb. 12:1). Without it, we cannot become mature in Christ. The term "perfect" in verse 4 is the common New Testament expression for maturity. And ultimately, without it, we will not obtain a full reward. Interestingly, the phrase "not deficient in anything" is built of the same Greek root word as is the term "inheritance."

Let some closing comments from the apostle Paul help reinforce the idea of this chapter. In Romans 5:1-5, he tells us about our new standing before God, "Therefore, since we have been declared righteous by faith, we have peace with God through our Lord Jesus Christ" (v. 1). He then says that through our relationship with Christ, we have "obtained access by faith into this grace in which we stand, and we rejoice in the hope of God's glory" (v. 2).

We can all appreciate the position we enjoy in the sphere of God's grace and the provisions of His grace that sustain us day by day. And we all rejoice greatly in the confidence that we will one day share in His glory. But Paul does not stop there. He now states the same truth that James and Peter told us about. Namely, that "… we also rejoice in sufferings, knowing…" (v. 3a). The Greek term for tribulations is *thlipsis*, and refers to the "sufferings, hard distressful circumstances." Rejoice over the stress and pressure of my job? You've got to be kidding! No, he is not kidding. And the reason is because we are expected to know something – "… that suffering (distressful circumstances) produces endurance" (v. 3b).

Wow! Distressful circumstances (the stresses and pressures of life) are what James would refer to as "all sorts of trials." And we would understand that Paul does not mean that these things, in themselves, produce endurance, but rather, that a *proper response* to them produces endurance. By the way, this is the same word (Gr. *hupomonē*) that James uses. To Paul, handling stress and pressure successfully (on the basis of faith) produces steadfast endurance. To James, our faith is proven when we handle the various trials of life successfully (on the basis of faith), and as a result, steadfast endurance is produced.

Notice the progression that follows: "and endurance, (produces) character, and character, hope. And hope does not disappoint" (vv. 4-5). Isn't this the same progression that James wrote about? Doesn't the salvation of our soul involve a process of growth in faith? Aren't we really being trained and matured like children?

4

It's for Your Own Good!

When we encounter trials and tests of our faith, whether suddenly or – as in everyday life – regularly, James says that we are to consider it as "nothing but joy." In making that assertion he assumes a certain frame of reference. First, *that we understand the dynamic relationship between the tests of our faith and maturity;* and secondly, *that our maturity in Christ relates to our inheritance in Christ.*

In the case of personal growth, to become a mature person requires training and development through a growth process that will take one from being an immature babe to a fully mature, productive adult. The process requires parental oversight and guidance. And both the Scriptures and experience teach us that the process can be quite an ordeal!

The Proverbs tell us that children are naturally foolish. Solomon put it this way: "Folly is bound up in the heart of the child" (Prov. 22:15). In general they are rebellious and require discipline. In fact, the second half of verse fifteen tells us "but the rod of discipline will drive it (foolishness) far from him."

Because children are foolish, they very often do not listen to the wisdom and instruction of their parents. The American author Mark Twain made a good point of this when he wrote, "When I was a boy of fourteen, my father was so ignorant I could hardly stand to have the old man around. But when I got to be twenty-one, I was astonished at how much he had learned in seven years."

It happens in the spiritual realm as well. Both the Old and New Testaments are replete with metaphors that picture God as a loving Father faithfully training His children. The point is so clear it does not need to be argued. Even the process and methods that he uses to train us are spelled out. Do you know what they are? Have you ever tried to relate the events of your life to this growth process? Do you see a relationship between the momentary tests of your faith that James talks about and God's overall training program? How about the stress and pressure that Paul speaks about in Romans 5:3 – how does that fit into the process?

Learning from Past Experiences

The Jewish Christians who lived in and around Jerusalem really had it rough. Imagine being raised in a culture dominated by the Law of Moses, where strict conformity to Mosaic legislation was expected – and even demanded. Imagine yourself identifying with a new religious group that was considered to be anti-Jewish and anti-Law of Moses, a group that believed its leader to be the promised Messiah. Your boss has told you that you are no longer needed. The shops in town no longer want to do business with you. You and your family are treated as outcasts from society.

You are not alone in your experience. Many others have also chosen to follow the Lord Jesus Christ as their Messiah. Many of them have experienced the seizure of their properties; some have even been thrown into prison. For a good while now you and the others have accepted your tribulations joyfully. You have tried to help each other the best you could. The Apostle Paul has also been a great help. Not long ago he was able to raise a large amount of money from among your gentile brethren. It certainly helped a lot of people.

But "enough is enough!" you say. "Surely Jesus should have returned by this time, it's been thirty years!" "How long must we endure these hardships?"

A short time later you begin to notice that some of your friends in the church are no longer there when you meet. You've heard that they've gone back to the old system. Maybe that's not a bad idea. Surely you would be welcomed back. Your old boss may be so glad to see you come to your senses that he might give you back your old job. You won't stop believing in Jesus as your Messiah and Savior, you reason, you'll just go through the motions of the Law. You might even lead some of them to believe in Christ!

What I have just described is the situation of the recipients of the letter to the Hebrews. In the letter the writer argues that what they are defecting from is far superior to what they are going back to. Jesus Christ is superior revelation (1:1-4); He is superior to Angels, beings held in high regard by the Jews (1:5-2:18); He is superior to Moses the Law-giver (3:1-6); He is superior to Aaron the Law-interpreter (4:14ff); and His priesthood is superior to that of the old Jewish order (7:1-28). He demonstrates the superiority of the work of Christ by contrasting the New Covenant with the Old (8:1-13); the New Sanctuary with the Old (9:1-10); and the New Sacrifice with the Old (9:11-10:18).

But carefully woven within his argument is a picture that is intended to bring fear to the hearts of the strongest of men. Simply stated, the picture is this: those who are believers in Christ are obligated to live in faithful obedience to the directives of the New Covenant. Just because the penalty of our sin was borne by Christ on the cross does not mean that there are no consequences for sin. Just as the children of Israel forfeited their inheritance because of unbelief – "the message they heard did them no good, since they did not join in with those who heard it in faith" (Heb. 4:2), we face that same possibility. It can happen to us the same way it happened to them. Thus the writer warns, "See to it, brothers and sisters, that none of you has an evil unbelieving heart that forsakes the living God" (3:12).

But what are we to do? "Exhort one another each day, ... that none of you may become hardened by sin's deception" (3:13). The Hebrews had failed. At the beginning their works of faith demonstrated an obedient walk with God. But now there are no works of faith. And there is no steadfast endurance (remember that James and Paul have said that steadfast endurance comes about as a result of an obedient faith). Even under the Old Covenant believers endured great hardship – including the loss of life – in order to lay hold of the promise (Heb. 11). What about you? Have the stress and pressure, afflictions and sufferings of life caused you to become disoriented to the plan of God? That's what happened to the Hebrews.

Some years ago I took flying lessons to obtain a pilots license. During the course of the instruction, I was taught (by demonstration) how easy it is to become disoriented in flight when you do not have an outside object with which to orient yourself – like when flying through a bank of clouds. It is possible to believe that you are ascending when in fact you are descending. You may believe that you are flying right-side up when really you are up-side down. The only way to survive is to trust your instruments. No matter what your senses tell you, you must trust your instruments.

The Hebrews became disoriented "flying through the clouds of life." They were "flying" according to their senses. They never checked the "instruments" – God's Word!

32

A Proper Orientation

"Therefore, since we are surrounded by such a great cloud of witnesses, we must get rid of every weight and the sin that clings so closely, and run with endurance the race set out for us, keeping our eyes fixed on Jesus, the pioneer and perfecter of our faith. For the joy set out for him he endured the cross, disregarding its shame, and has taken his seat at the right hand of the throne of God." (Heb. 12:1-2).

"Don't let anything keep you from the finish line," the writer says. "Many others have done it, and you can too. But to make it takes endurance, and you must keep your eyes firmly fixed on the finish line. Great reward awaits those who run the race successfully." But then, if it is so simple, what happened to the Hebrews? They forgot something!

What they forgot is at once both simple and profound: "And have you have forgotten the exhortation addressed to you as sons? 'My son, do not scorn the Lord's discipline or give up when he corrects you. For the Lord disciplines the one he loves and chastises every son he accepts'" (12:5). It is a quote from Proverbs 3:11-12. Everything they were experiencing in life was related to this statement. They had failed to orient themselves on the basis of it. Their regression from maturity back to being babes again (5:11-6:12), their lack of steadfast endurance, and their potential loss of inheritance, all resulted from a lack of application of this truth!

God is training us as His children. Everything we experience in life is a part of that training process. It is the very same thing James and Paul spoke about. The circumstances of our lives (stress, pressure, tests of faith) are intended to mature our faith and equip us to receive our inheritance. They accomplish that as long as we handle them correctly. And it is our works of faith that prove whether or not we are handling them correctly (cf. James 2). It is because of this growth process that the writer states, "Endure your sufferings as discipline; God is treating you as sons" (12:7).

Words Are Important

The English words of these verses don't tell the full story. For example, take the word *discipline*. We tend to think in terms of the rod, or a belt. But the Greek word *paideia* (discipline) means far more than that. It refers to the whole training and education of children. It involves the cultivation of mind and morals. It employs admonition, reproof, and punishment. In this context it is best understood as God's *training program*.

The phrase *give up* is actually one word in the original text (Gr. *ekluō*) and means to become despondent or fainthearted, and the term *corrects* (Gr. *elegchō*) means to convict or point out a fault. Another important term is *chastises* (Gr. *mastigoō*) which means chastening and training by affliction. With these definitions in mind, let's develop a paraphrase of the text:

My son, do not take lightly the training program of the Lord, nor become despondent or fainthearted when He points out areas in your life that need work, for those whom the Lord loves He trains as His children, and He chastens and trains by affliction every son whom He receives.

Do you see the point? Everything that we face in life is a part of God's training program for us as His children. There are no exceptions! And it is through this training program that we are matured and prepared to receive our inheritance. There is no other program. In its outworking, God affirms the character of our faith as well as pointing out those areas that need work. The same circumstances can do both together. Further, God does not give up on us; He is faithful to the task.

Keep in mind, however, that the experience of it is not always pleasant. Nor is it intended to be. We may be called upon to face loneliness, sorrow, illness, pain and heartache, even death. And we are reminded that "All discipline seems painful at the time, not joyful" (12:11a). But if we hang in there with faith and obedience, and with the high expectation which faith brings, it will accomplish the objective: "But later it produces the fruit of peace and righteousness for those who are trained by it" (12:11b).

5

Look Out for the Enemy!

As if the growth process were not difficult enough by itself – now we have to learn that someone is working overtime to keep us from the goal! Listen to this: "Be sober and alert. Your enemy the devil, like a roaring lion, is on the prowl looking for someone to devour" (1 Peter 5:8).

Sounds intimidating – even frightening, doesn't it? Right now you might be asking yourself, "What chance do I really have of becoming fully mature or adequately prepared to receive my inheritance in Christ? I'm no match for Satan!" Yes and no. If you remain spiritually immature, you are right, you are no match for Satan. But on the other hand, if you cooperate with God's training program and live in faithful obedience to the directives of His Word, then you have every reason to expect to be victorious over the "roaring lion"!

In Ephesians 4:11-16, the apostle Paul addresses the process that God uses to equip us for growth. That process is essentially this: evangelists and pastors and teachers, through instruction and training, equip believers for the work of ministry, all with a view to the building up or maturing of the Body of Christ.

Every Christian has an intended role in the process. Using the metaphor of a human body, Christ is likened to the head, while the individual believers correspond to its various joints and parts. It is described this way: *"We will in all things grow up into Christ, who is the head. From him the whole body grows, fitted and held together through every supporting ligament. As each one does its part, the body grows in love"* (vv.16, 17). This maturity process will continue until *"we all attain ... to a mature person, attaining to the measure of Christ's full stature"* (v.13).

We can expect that if we are faithfully involved in the process, we will be progressing toward becoming a fully mature, productive adult. No longer will we remain children. But what if we harden our hearts and the Word becomes unprofitable in our lives – like it did in the case of the Hebrew Christians (see Hebrews, chapter four)? What happens if we remain children or regress back to being children (see 1 Cor. 2:14-3:3; Heb. 5:11-14)?

As a consequence of becoming spiritually mature, God's Word says that "we are no longer to be children" (Eph. 4:14a). But if we do not become mature, we will remain children. And Paul describes what children are like: they are "tossed back and forth by waves and carried about by every wind of teaching by the trickery of people who craftily carry out their deceitful schemes" (Eph. 4:14b). Quite a picture! Children are unstable and easily led astray.

The term *craftily* is particularly instructive. It is translated from the Greek word *kubeia*, which is used only once in the entire New Testament. The word involves the concept of *throwing dice*. Perhaps we can understand its intended meaning if we paraphrase the passage:

> As a result of our becoming mature Christians we will no longer be children. Children are like a ship caught in a storm at sea, which is tossed here and there by waves – by every new idea and teaching that comes along! They don't understand that they are being tricked and led astray from the truth. To put it bluntly, Christians who are uncooperative in

God's training program, and thus remain children, are like those who "shoot craps" with the devil – and he has "loaded dice" – there is no way they can win against him!"

The conflict between Satan (we'll use this name to refer to the devil and his demons), and the believer is commonly referred to as *spiritual warfare*. What is spiritual warfare all about? How can we be victorious, not led astray so as to remain immature and ultimately forfeit our inheritance in Christ? Let's take a look.

What Spiritual Conflict Is All About

There are two kingdoms currently functioning on earth: the kingdom of darkness and the kingdom of light – the latter being referred to in Colossians 1:13 as "the kingdom of the Son he loves."

The kingdom of darkness is made up of spirit beings who are called variously in Scripture by the terms: evil spirits, demons, devils, principalities, powers, rulers of darkness, et al. All unsaved human beings are also a part of this kingdom, and Satan rules as its king.

The kingdom of light is made up of the righteous. That is, the unfallen angels and saved human beings, with the Lord Jesus Christ reigning as king.

The Bible pictures these two kingdoms in conflict. The human beings in the kingdom of darkness are said to be spiritually dead (see Eph. 2:1). They do not possess eternal life – which involves both a relationship with God and a quality of existence. They are incapable of thinking God's thoughts – having neither the desire nor the capacity to do so (see Rom. 8:7; 1 Cor. 2:1-16). Because they reject God and have no desire to know or serve Him, they ascribe greater worth and value to the creation than to God (see Rom. 1:25). Too, since they have not been freed from sin by faith in Christ, they are still enslaved to it. Consequently, they live to gratify their fleshly impulses and desires. They are totally self-serving (see Eph. 4:17-19).

The various philosophies of this world system – which is a manifestation of the kingdom of darkness, are nothing more than an articulation of its understanding of life and how it is to be lived. Being void of God's viewpoint, it represents man's best efforts to describe what has been, what is, and what shall be. Ultimately, the philosophies of this world's system are attributable to Satan, who is said to be "the god of this age" (see 2 Cor. 4:4).

The warfare between the kingdom of darkness and the kingdom of light is said not to be "according to human standards" (lit. *according to the flesh*, 2 Cor. 10:3). It is *spiritual* warfare (see Eph. 6:12). However, that is not to say that its outworking does not involve the issues of the flesh (physical), for the Scriptures make it certain that it does.

Whereas the Bible makes it very clear that Satan cannot possess a believer – there is not one biblical example of this ever happening, a believer can be taken captive in the war. And because of satanic brainwashing, some will actually come under the control of Satan – ultimately being used by him against the kingdom of light!

In Colossians 2:8, the Apostle Paul issues a stern warning when he says, "Be careful not to allow anyone to captivate you." The term *captivate* (Gr. *sulagōgeō*) has the idea of being carried off as spoil or booty in a war, as a prisoner of war. But this only begs the question: How is it possible for a believer to become a prisoner of war? Paul says it is by being captivated *through an empty, deceitful philosophy that is according to human traditions and the elemental spirits of the world, and not according to Christ."*

When a believer embraces the thinking of the world, he has been had! And the enemy is very skilled in the way he presents his argument. He knows how to take the tenants of humanistic psychology and mix in a little Scripture to take an unsuspecting believer down the wrong path. He knows how to use the media to represent life in a way so as to challenge one's moral value system. And when the believer buys into these arguments and modifies his worldview accordingly, he becomes an agent for the enemy – simply because he begins to propagate the same views to which he has now become captive!

This is, indeed, a very serious condition. In fact, it is so serious that it will take God's direct intervention to free a person from it. A clear example of this is presented in 2 Timothy 2:24-26. The instructions begin by describing the manner in which a godly person should minister the Word to someone in a captured state: "And the Lord's slave must not engage in heated disputes but be kind toward all, an apt teacher, patient, correcting opponents with gentleness" (vv.24-25a).

Now, an important question is this: Why is it so important to be careful to minister the Word in this manner? The answer follows in the text: "Perhaps God will grant them repentance [a change of thinking] and then knowledge of the truth" (v.25b). This makes it very clear that their release from being held captive to these philosophies ultimately depends upon God. Notice the final phrase in verse twenty-six: "And they will come to their senses and escape the devil's trap where they are held captive to do his will."

Before we continue, let me state emphatically once again that there is not one biblical example of a believer

ever being what is commonly called "demon possessed." There are examples of believers being *influenced, controlled* (the term "filled" conveys the notion of "control and domination"), and *harassed* by satanic forces (see Acts 5:3; 2 Cor. 12:7). Sometimes believers are given over to Satan for discipline (see 1 Cor. 5:5), but even in that case there is no indication that they are ever "indwelt" or "possessed" by him. To put it another way, Satan's work against us is based from without, not from within.

How Satan Operates

When it comes to spiritual warfare, the first thing that we need to understand is that we are totally responsible for our own choices. If we think, say or do something, it is because we have chosen to do so. Satan cannot force us to do anything against our will. Second, we need to realize that the battleground for spiritual warfare is *the mind*. Paul makes this very clear in 2 Cor. 10:3-5: "For though we live by human standards, we do not wage war according to human standards, for the weapons of our warfare are not human weapons, but are made powerful by God for tearing down strongholds. We tear down arguments and every arrogant obstacle that is raised up against the knowledge of God, and we take every thought captive and make it obey Christ."

This is the most neglected area for most Christians. Although we are instructed to renew our minds on the Word of God (see Romans 12:2 – this being the way *not* to be conformed to this world system), most spend very little time in the process. How can we recognize error if we do not know the truth? How can we recognize and refute the empty philosophies of this world if we do not have a biblical worldview? The most common result is being "tossed back and forth by waves and carried about

LOOK OUT FOR THE ENEMY!!

by every wind of teaching by the trickery of people who craftily carry out their deceitful schemes" (Eph. 4:14b).

The methodology of Satan is deceit and fraud (cf. Rev. 12:9; 1 Tim. 4:1). In Acts 13:5-10, we have a record of Paul's encounter with a man representing the kingdom of darkness. Paul was reasoning with the proconsul at Salamis, Sergius Paulus, who is said to be "an intelligent man" (v.7). However, a man called Elymus "opposed them, trying to turn the proconsul away from the faith" (v.8). Paul's rebuke of Elymus provides clear insight into how Satan operates in the war. "Paul, filled with the Holy Spirit, stared straight at him and said, 'You who are full of all **deceit** and **wrongdoing** (unscrupulousness or fraud), you son of the devil, you enemy of all righteousness – **will you not stop making crooked the straight paths of the Lord?**'" (Vv.9-10, emphasis mine). What Paul was involved in with Elymus is exactly what he stated in 2 Cor. 10:3-5.

Satan, through deceit and fraud, attacks the Word of God with the goal of getting those in the Kingdom of Light to rebel against their King. If and to whatever extent he is successful, he actually gets those in the Kingdom of Light to obey him. In that sense they are under his control. Do not miss the main point: *the battle is waged in the mind*. If we do not have a clear biblical worldview, we are vulnerable to deception and fraud. We will readily then buy into Satan's worldview, for it will sound right (make sense)! It may even be – and often is – presented as biblical doctrine!

But not only is our weakened mind a problem, but our flesh is weak also. This is an additional area of vulnerability. When we become believers in the Lord Jesus Christ, we receive forgiveness for all our sins. God declares us "not guilty" because Christ died for our sins. Romans 6 informs us that whereas we were previously enslaved to sin, now, in Christ, we have been set free from its power in our lives. In other words, we are free *not* to obey the lusts of our flesh. But we can still do so *if we choose* to! That is why the appeal of Scripture is to my mind and volition – "So you too **consider** yourselves dead to sin, but alive to God in Christ Jesus. Therefore **do not let** sin reign in your mortal body so that you obey its desires, and **do not present** your members to sin as instruments to be used for unrighteousness, but **present** yourselves to God as those who are alive from the dead and your members to God as instruments to be used for righteousness" (Rom. 6:11-13, emphasis mine).

We still have a problem with sin. Our flesh is still with us. We are no longer enslaved to it, but we have the continuing capacity to satisfy its lusts – if we choose to! The strategy of Satan is to try to get us who are now in the Kingdom of Light to rebel against God and His Word, and to gratify the lusts of our flesh.

Areas Subject To Attack

1 John 2:16 lists three areas in which Satan mounts his attack, "Because all that is in the world (**the desire of the flesh and the desire of the eyes and the arrogance produced by material possessions**), is not from the Father, but is from the world" (emphasis mine). These are the things that are important to those in the Kingdom of Darkness. They are captive to the lusts of the flesh. They are driven by materialistic desires. They want to be somebody! Their philosophy of life is totally (to borrow a word from their own system) narcissistic – having an excessive admiration of one's self.

Satan approached our Lord in this same way. In our day, Satan uses the people in his kingdom (they are enslaved to their adamic nature and to the philosophies of this world), and especially its media to appeal to our capacity to leave God out. He makes it sound so good. We can be happy, fulfilled, powerful, and rich – and feel really good, if we will just do things his way. Perhaps a diagram of our Lord's temptation will help. The particulars are recorded in Matthew 4:1-11.

AREA	APPEAL	RESPONSE
Desire of the flesh	Physical needs "Turn stones to bread"	"It is written"
Desire of the eyes	Wealth "Kingdoms of the world"	"It is written"
Arrogant pride	Accomplishments/ Power/Etc. "Cast yourself down"	"It is written"

Satan operates the same way with us. And we are to respond the same way that Jesus responded, on the basis of the Word of God. One additional comment with regard to the desire of the flesh and the desire of the eyes and the arrogance produced by material possessions: because our flesh craves satisfaction, we have natural bends and desires in that direction. Those of the Kingdom of Darkness can only make their appeal to these areas. We are the ones who choose to satisfy them in inappropriate ways. We are totally responsible! No one in the Kingdom of Light is justified making the claim, "The devil made me do it!"

Some Concluding Thoughts

Satan and those of his kingdom will try to influence us by presenting arguments that are deceptive and untrue. They will try to convince us that we need certain things, that we must dress a certain way, smell a certain way, look a certain way, talk a certain way, believe a certain way, behave a certain way, drive certain cars, live in certain neighborhoods, have relationships with certain people, etc. (the list is endless), if we are going to fit in, be somebody, and experience a full and meaningful life.

We cannot be dominated or controlled by satanic seductions, or by the flesh, or the pride of life apart from our own choices, but I am not sure that the average Christian has the discernment to tell whether he is a victor or a victim in the conflict. However, the Word of God does provide us with a strategy for victory. We are to "take every thought captive to make it obey Christ." This is what makes it possible for us to "tear down arguments and every arrogant obstacle raised up against the knowledge of God" (2 Cor. 10:5). We are also to "take up the full armor of God so that you may be able to stand your ground on the evil day, and having done everything, to stand" (Eph. 6:13). We are further told to "Resist the devil and he will flee from you" (James 4:7). Preeminent is the command found in the first part of James 4:7 – the real key to victory: "So submit to God."

Life is serious business. We have nothing to fear as long as we walk with Christ. We cannot be victorious over the world, the flesh or the devil by living in the strength of our flesh. It is only as we continue to renew our minds through God's Word and walk in the power of His Spirit so as to experience victory and enjoy the eternal life that is ours in Christ.

6

Living Under the Right Influence

Perhaps the most important concept that a believer must understand in the sanctification process is how his thinking is related to the biblical concept of spiritual maturity. Spirituality by definition is a grown-up and growing relation to the Holy Spirit.[1] And while this may simply be another way of saying that spirituality is Christian maturity, what this definition tries to do is to delineate more openly the factors of spiritual growth over a period of time.

What is spirituality?

Genuine spirituality involves three things. First, it involves regeneration, for no one can be spiritual who is not been made alive by the Spirit at the point of trusting in Christ for their salvation. Regeneration is the first essential in spirituality.

The second is that the Holy Spirit is preeminently involved in producing spirituality. The entire growth process takes place under the filling of the Spirit. To be filled with the Spirit means to be influenced and controlled by the Spirit so that the thought-life, speech and behavior of the person will reflect the character of God.

The third element involved in the concept of spirituality is time. If, according to 1 Corinthians 2:15, the spiritual person has the ability to appraise [judge] the quality or worth of all things, this must involve time in order to

---

[1] Charles C. Ryrie, Balancing the Christian Life, p.13

gain the knowledge and experience necessary to be able to appraise all things. The word maturity, therefore, seems to hold the key to this whole concept of spirituality, for Christian maturity is the growth that the Holy Spirit produces in the life of a believer over a period of time. It is important also to note that the amount of time necessary for maturity is not the same for every person, but some time is necessary for all.

When I took physics in high school, I learned a basic formula that many of us use when we are taking a trip in an automobile. We use it to calculate how long it's going to take us to get from where we are to where we want to be. The formula is rate times time equals distance. If you drive 50 mph for 3 hours, you will have driven 150 miles. Lower your rate of speed and it will take you longer to reach the same distance.

The same principle is also true when applied to the spiritual realm. The rate has to do with our intake and application of the Word of God; the distance is the goal of maturity. How long will it take to reach our goal? If we increase the rate then it takes less time to reach the goal. If our rate slows down, it takes us a longer time to get to the goal. The extreme would also be true: the goal will never be reached if there is no rate!

Consider the two classifications of people that are in the world. 1 Corinthians 2:14 describes the first classification: the *natural* man. Notice that it says of him that he "does not receive the things of the Spirit of God, for they are foolishness to him. And he cannot understand them, because they are spiritually discerned." This person is clearly to be classified as an unbeliever. He wants nothing to do with God; the things of God are foolish to him; he is devoid of the Spirit [spiritually dead], thus being unable to understand the things of God.

The second classification is noted in verse 15, where the natural man is contrasted with one who is called the *spiritual* man. The fact that he is called spiritual gives clear indication that he is a believer in Christ, one that has been regenerated by the Holy Spirit. The text says that he "discerns all things," and yet he himself is "understood by no man." The Living Bible translates the phrase like this: "He just baffles the man of the world." And the reason is because someone who is not spiritually minded just cannot understand how a spiritually minded person ticks – because their worldview, their frame of reference, is so different. And yet being able to see things from God's point of view, the spiritual man has the ability to judge the quality or worth of all things.

All people fall into one of these two categories: they are either believers or they are unbelievers. But in the case of believers – and we will develop this in a moment – there are actually three conditions in which they can be found, the spiritual person being the first.

A popular understanding of the spiritual man has evolved over the last 50 years or so, primarily because of a little volume that was published by the first president and founder of Dallas Seminary, Louis Sperry Chafer. The book is entitled, *He That is Spiritual*. What Chafer postulated in that book is basically this: spirituality is relative and maturity is absolute. Chafer understood spirituality and maturity, although related, as being distinct. He understood being filled with the Spirit as a state of being. Utilizing 1 John 1:9 as a basis he said if there is no unconfessed sin in your life, you are filled with the Spirit. For many it has become nothing more than a mechanical formula: no unconfessed sin in your life, you are filled with the Spirit. When you sin, confess it and you are immediately filled with the Spirit.

Chafer's view was picked up by some of his students who later were instrumental in developing materials used in the ministries of such well-known organizations as Campus Crusade for Christ, whose presentation of the Spirit-filled life is essentially the same as that of Chafer.

It is important to note that there is no reference anywhere in the New Testament to any sort of formula to confess your sins in order to be filled with Spirit. The point is this: Chafer's view of the Spirit-filled life is not correct biblically and I'm going to show you why.

Recall what the spiritual person is able to do. He is able to discern all things. That is the exact opposite from the unbeliever who does not want anything to do with the things of God. He does not have the ability to discern all things.

The circumstance of the believers in the book of Hebrews will give us insight into the problem. The Hebrews were believers living in and around Jerusalem just prior to the destruction of Jerusalem in 70 A.D. They had grown to a place of maturity but because of the neglect of the Word of God, they had regressed back to a place of being babies again – which introduces another basic principle: We can grow to a place of maturity in our relationship with Christ and then regress back to being a baby again. There is no maintaining the status quo; you cannot grow to a certain level of maturity, cool your heels for a while, and then pick up where you left off. You are either moving forward or you are moving backward at any given time.

In Hebrews 5:11 the writer is beginning to address the doctrine of the priesthood of Melchizedek but realizes that he has a problem because of the maturity level of his audience. He begins by saying, "on this topic" – that is,

Melchizedek – "we have much to say and it is difficult to explain, since you have become sluggish in hearing."

Notice he does not say, "You are sluggish in hearing." He says, "You have become sluggish in hearing." This phrase and the phrases that follow, "you have gone back to needing" clearly indicate a regression from a previous state.

He continues: "For though you should in fact be teachers by this time, you again need someone to teach you the beginning elements of God's utterances. You have gone back to needing milk, not solid food." Did you pick up on what he said? "You have gone back to needing milk, not solid food." He explains further: "For everyone who lives on milk is inexperienced in the message of righteousness." Why? "Because he is an infant."

Note carefully that the baby Christian feeds on milk, not solid food. That is his diet. "But solid food," he says, "is for the mature, whose perceptions are trained by practice" – that is, by living out the word of God in life. For what purpose? "To discern both good and evil." My friend, that is the same characteristic as that of the Spiritual man in 1 Corinthians 2:15. He has the ability to discern all things. It is absolutely clear: *the spiritual man is a mature Christian!*

Now, let's go back to 1 Corinthians 3:1 and see how this spiritual person of 2:15 carries over into this verse. In 3:1 Paul says, "So, brothers and sisters, I could not speak to you as spiritual people, but instead as people of the flesh, as to infants in Christ." This verse moves us into the second condition in which we may find believers that are in the world: those who are referred to as being "people of the flesh." But there are two sub-categories of fleshliness. The first one is called *fleshly* because he is a infant in Christ. Notice from verse 1 that this person is contrasted with the spiritual person of 2:15.

When a person is a brand-new believer in Christ, his lifestyle is characteristically fleshly simply because he doesn't know any different. His thinking – and remember that as we think within ourselves that's the way we are – his core beliefs, are based on something other than the Word of God. Therefore, fleshliness doesn't mean that a person is necessarily involved in a lot of immorality, drunkenness, murder, and things like that, although that could be a part of it; but basically a fleshly person is one who does not live according to the word of God.

The world is full of Ph.D.s who are fools. A fool by definition is not an unintelligent person. A fool by definition is one who chooses to persist in a worldview that has nothing or little to do with God. That's why the Bible tells us that heavenly wisdom and earthly wisdom are different (see James 3:13-18). Skills in living life differ according to the character that is attendant to the wisdom. There is a heavenly wisdom; there is an earthly wisdom. The same concept is involved here. An infant is fleshly simply because he has not had enough time to renew his mind on the word of God so as to think differently. He thinks just like the world. You would expect that of a infant, right?

And according to Hebrews 5:11-14, infants feed on what? Milk. So its no surprise that Paul brings that into play here. He continues by saying, "I fed you milk, not solid food, for you were not yet ready." Why? They were infants in Christ. Remember, solid food is for the mature.

In this passage, Paul is actually revisiting the time when he founded the church in mid-March of 51 A.D. It is now the summer of 56 A.D. Five years have passed. One would have expected infants to grow up. But what do we see? Listen to this, "In fact, you are still not ready, for you are still influenced by the flesh." This brings us to the problem of those who persist in being children. Just because a person is a believer in the Lord Jesus Christ does not mean that the passing of time in itself is going to produce maturity. Remember the formula: rate times time equal distance. If distance equals maturity and rate equals the intake and application of the Word of God, then time by itself doesn't produce anything. You cannot reach the goal of maturity without being involved in the rate to get there.

So, there are two conditions in which we find believers who are in the world. First, there is the mature believer, who in 1 Corinthians 2:15 is called *spiritual*. This same person in Hebrews 5:14 is called *mature*. The second condition is called *fleshly*. But there are two subclasses of fleshly: One is a infant, a brand new or relatively new believer. The other is a believer who has persisted in being a child – he has refused to be involved in the process of growing up. As a result, his thinking is essentially the same as that of an infant Christian, and his life is influenced and controlled by that thinking. The conclusion that we can draw is this: the spiritual man is not just one who is spirit-filled – for that can be the momentary (but not characteristic) experience even of a baby Christian; the spiritual man is one who is a *mature* believer.

The key item in all of this is this, of course, is the role of the Holy Spirit in the growth of the believer. In Ephesians 5:15 and following, Paul begins by saying that we need to be careful how we walk. The preceding couple of paragraphs in this chapter are important because the "therefore" in verse 15 is drawing an application from what went before it. In essence he has said this: we are no longer darkness; we are light. Therefore, we are to live like it. We are not to be partakers in the unfruitful works of darkness, but rather we are to expose them.

It makes sense, then, that he would now say, "be very careful how you live – not as unwise but as wise, taking advantage of every opportunity, because the days are evil." There is so much vying for our time that we must choose wisely how we will use our time in order to accomplish the objectives that God has given to us.

A basic principle of time management is this: *If you don't control your time, other people will control it for you.* Do you know that principle? A lot of people seem to think that because they do not have anything to do, that you do not either. They drop by, call you on the phone, etc., just to chat – and it seldom has any substance to it at all. If you don't control your time, other people will control it for you.

In verse 17 Paul continues by saying, "For this reason do not be foolish." In this context, the proper utilization of time is evidence of either wise or foolish living. Further, to live wisely one must understand that God's will for every believer is "not [to] get drunk with wine, which is debauchery, but be filled by the spirit" (verse 18).

Now the contrast between getting drunk and being filled by the spirit is really important. If you were to drink alcohol to the point that you were under its influence and you were driving a car and a policeman saw your car moving about erratically and pulled you over, what kind of summons would he give you? DWI or DUI. What does it mean? You are driving while intoxicated, or driving under the influence. And that is really the key to understanding the Spirit-filled life. Instead of being under the influence of something like alcohol, we are to live under the influence of the Holy Spirit. Which brings us to the meaning of *filled.*

54

What does it mean to be filled with the Spirit?

There are two Greek words that are important to understand when talking about being filled with the Spirit. The first word is *pimplēmi* and the other is *plēroō*. Both of these terms are very similar, but there is also a critical difference between them. They both have a literal and a metaphorical use. The literal sense means to fill up something with something. For example, in Luke 5:5-7 the term *pimplēmi* is used in a literal sense: "Master, we worked hard all night and caught nothing! But at your word I will lower the nets. When they had done this, they caught so many fish that their nets started to tear. So they motioned to their partners in the other boat to come and help them. And they came and filled both boats, so that they were about to sink." So filling the boats with fish is an example of *pimplēmi* being used in the literal sense – of filling something with something. Do you see?

Now turn to John 12. Jesus is in the home of Mary, Martha and Lazarus and they were having supper together. In verse 3 it says, "Then Mary took three quarters of a pound of expensive aromatic oil of pure nard and anointed the feet of Jesus. She then wiped his feet with her hair. (Now the house was filled with the fragrance of the perfumed oil.)" Here, the term *plēroō* is translated filled and shows how it also can be used in a literal sense.

If I had a big pitcher in my hand and I filled it with water, that is the meaning of both words when used in a literal sense. But when you use them as a figure of speech, metaphorically, they take on different connotations. In a metaphorical sense, they both mean this: to influence, to control. It means that what fills you will be that which influences and controls your life – your thoughts, your words, and your actions. In other words, you will be living under its influence and control. Like

55

the wine in the Ephesians 5:18 passage, whatever influences and controls your life will be observed in your life in behavioral ways.

To see the metaphorical use of these same terms, let's look at a couple of passages where the filling of the Spirit is *not* being illustrated. In this way we will be better able to grasp the concept of the words.

In Luke 4:25-30, we have the account of Jesus' ministry in Nazareth and the people's response to it – which was not at all pleasant! In verse 28 we read, "all the people in the synagogue were filled with rage." This is a metaphorical use of *pimplēmi*. If the sense is whatever fills (influences and controls) a person will be evidenced by their behavior, we should expect to see some behavioral expression in the context. And indeed we do. Notice verse 29, "They got up, forced him out of the town, and brought him to the brow of the hill on which their town was built, so that they could throw him down the cliff."

Plēroō can be illustrated in the same way. In Acts 5, a large segment of the people were turning to the apostles for instruction and leadership as they ministered the word of God. As a result, the church was developing and expanding. The religious leaders of the Jews become jealous and envious of the ministry of the apostles. In verse 17 we are told "Now the high priest rose up, and all those with him (that is, the religious party of the Sadducees), and they were filled with jealousy." Jealousy is now in control of their lives. The result? "They laid hands on the apostles and put them in a public jail."

Do you see how strongly emotions can control a person's behavior? That is what *being filled* means when used in a metaphorical sense: whatever fills you will manifest itself behaviorally in your life.

56

Most uses of these terms in the New Testament, when not referring to the filling of the Spirit, refer to emotions. And you remember where emotions come from, do you not? Of course you do; they come from our thinking. We think and analyze life momentarily and emotions are generated. And those emotions have a tremendous influence on our behavior – the things we say and do.

Civil law recognizes this. Do we not have laws that fall under the category of "crimes of passion"? Recently I noticed a headline story at the bottom of page one in the paper about road rage. Think just for a quick moment about road rage and what it is. At its core, it is the sin of selfishness.

Picture in your mind someone driving who is selfish in their beliefs about their rights and their space on the road. Suddenly, another driver cuts them off. They quickly analyze the situation based on their selfish beliefs and they become angry because this thoughtless, arrogant person has moved into *my* space! They speed up next to that person's car with a stern glare on their face, and as soon as the person looks their way, they wave to them in an unfriendly manner. They do not realize that their life is being greatly influenced and controlled by the emotion of anger; hence, road rage.

Sometimes in such circumstances people will shoot you. I mean, they will actually take out a gun and shoot you. There was an illustration in the same article about a person who shot up the car of another person – it even had some children in it – because the other person had cut over into *their* space.

Not long ago the controller for the city of Houston was in court charged with road rage because somebody violated *his* space. He got out of his car and punched the guy out on the side of the road. Can you believe it? What is it called? *Road rage!*

What was the problem? It began with a person's fundamental beliefs about himself, about the world in which he lives, in which his frame of reference, his worldview, influenced him to interpret the reality of the circumstance in a way that generated a very strong emotion. And that emotion was so strong that it influenced and controlled his behavior. What we see overtly is the result of it.

Take any emotion: anger, jealousy, envy, greed – any of these emotional feelings – they can influence and control your whole life. But the main point to see is this: whatever fills you; that is, whatever influences and controls your life, will demonstrate itself behaviorally in the way that you live.

In fact, we can say this: Our behavior – including our thoughts, words and actions – is a revelation of what consistently influences and controls our lives. Make sense? Let me say it again. When we look at our lives, our behavior and the words that come out of our mouth – what other people observe and hear – it is nothing more than an expression of what characteristically influences and controls our life. And that is true for every person.

What about the influence and control of the Holy Spirit? Consider Luke, chapter one, where we find two examples of individuals who are said to be under the influence [remember, this is what *being filled* means] of the Holy Spirit.

In verse fifteen, we are told how the future ministry of John the Baptist would be conducted: "He will be filled with the Holy Spirit, even before his birth." In other words, John's ministry would be conducted characteristically under the influence of the Holy Spirit. And what would be the results? Verse sixteen tells us that in part

"He will turn back the people of Israel to the Lord their God. He will go as forerunner before the Lord in the spirit and power of Elijah, to turn the hearts of the fathers back to their children and the disobedient to the wisdom of the just, to make ready for the Lord a people prepared for him."

In verses thirteen through sixteen, the angel Gabriel announced to Zacharias that he and his wife, Elizabeth, who were in advanced years of life, were going to have a child. Six months into her pregnancy, Elizabeth visits Mary, the mother of our Lord. Upon hearing Mary's greeting, the baby leaped in her womb and Elizabeth was filled with the Holy Spirit (v.41). That means that at that moment she was under the influence and control of the Holy Spirit. What is the result? Verse 42 tells us that "She exclaimed with a loud voice, 'Blessed are you among women, and blessed is the child in your womb! And who am I that the mother of my Lord should come and visit me?'" (vv.42-43). Elizabeth's declaration was the behavioral expression or result, at that moment, of her being under the influence and control of the Holy Spirit.

In the second chapter of Acts, we have the account of the coming of the Holy Spirit at Pentecost. The Apostles are the focal point of the narrative (the nearest antecedent for the pronoun *they* in verse one is the term *apostles* in 1:26). And while they were gathered together in one place, the text says that a *sound* was heard as if it were a violent, rushing wind. Further, it says "And tongues spreading out like fire appeared to them and came to rest on each of them (i.e., the apostles)" (v.3). Although it is not explicitly stated in the passage, we do know that it was at this time that the Holy Spirit came to indwell the apostles (the baptism of the Holy Spirit; see also 1 Cor. 12:13; and Peter's explanation in Acts 11:15-16).

Verse 4 tells us All of them (i.e., the apostles) were filled with the Holy Spirit." What result do we see? "And they began to speak in other languages as the Spirit enabled them." They were "speaking ... about the great deeds God has done" (v.11). We know that they were speaking known languages – not some kind of gibberish – because of the term *dialect* that is used in verses six and eight (translated as *language*). Another example is in Acts 4:8 where it says, "Then Peter, filled with the Holy Spirit, replied, 'Rulers of the people and elders, ...'" Peter's sermon was the result of his being filled (*pimplēmi*) with the Spirit.

After Paul's conversion, he was told by Ananias that "The Lord Jesus ... has sent me so that you may see again and be filled with the Holy Spirit" (Acts 9:17). And although the immediate result of that filling, if any, is not stated, it certainly has to do with the conduct of his ministry as an apostle.

The final example of *pimplēmi* used for the filling of the Spirit is found in Acts 13:9. The text says, "But Saul (also known as Paul), filled with the Holy Spirit, stared straight at him and said, 'You who are full of all deceit and all wrongdoing ...'" Paul's statement was the result of his being filled with the Spirit at that moment.

There is only one occasion where *plēroō* is used for the filling with the Spirit and that is Acts 13:52. It simply says, "And the disciples were filled with joy and the Holy Spirit."

In sum, let me mention some general observations and conclusions about these two terms. First, pimple,,mi is always seen as a sovereign act of God whereby He uses or influences a person so as to bring about a particular act of ministry – almost without exception, some ministry of the word.

I experience this kind of filling regularly in my ministry. Many times when I am teaching things come to my mind – not things that I have not known before, but things that I have known but had not planned in advance to say – and I know God is the one who has influenced my thinking because of the appropriateness of the thought at the time, or the related passages that come to my mind.

The second thing about *pimplēmi* is this: We are never directed in Scripture to be filled in this way. There is no directive either to seek after or to be filled in this way. It is a sovereign act of God in a person's life.

The only way that *pimplēmi* and *plēroō* differ is that we are directed to be filled with the Spirit in the *plēroō* sense (see Eph. 5:18). It will not take place unless we cooperate. Further, the tense of the verb suggests a continuing action – something that should be characteristic of our lives. But an important question is this: How do I allow the Holy Spirit to influence and control my life? And what results will be seen in my behavior if I allow Him to influence and control me?

What are the results of being filled with the spirit?

To answer these questions we first turn to the context of the directive, Ephesians 5:18. The passage says, "And do not get drunk with wine, which is debauchery, but be filled by the Spirit."

Following the command, various behaviors are described that indicate the results that issue from being filled with the Spirit: "speaking to one another in psalms, hymns, and spiritual songs, singing and making music in your hearts to the Lord, always giving thanks for all things in the name of our Lord Jesus Christ to God the Father for each other in the name of our Lord Jesus Christ, and submitting to one another out of reverence for Christ."

The final phrase, "submitting to one another out of reverence for Christ" (mutual submission in the Body), is then applied to differing relationships in the Church: "Wives, submit to your husbands"(5:22); "Husbands, love your wives" (5:25); "Children, obey your parents" (6:1); "Fathers, do not provoke your children to anger" (6:4); "Slaves, obey your human masters" (6:5); "Masters, treat your slaves the same way, giving up the use of threats" (6:9).

Let's look at a parallel passage where Paul is speaking about the same subject but in a slightly different way. The passage is Colossians 3:15-4:1. In 3:16, the directive is, "Let the word of Christ dwell in you richly" Now look at the results of that action: "Teaching and exhorting one another with all wisdom, singing psalms, hymns, and spiritual songs, all with grace in your hearts to God. And whatever you do in word or deed, do it all in the name of the Lord Jesus, giving thanks to God the Father through him." He then adds, "Wives, submit to your husbands" (3:18); "Husbands, love your wives" (3:19); "Children, obey your parents" (6:20); "Fathers, do not provoke your children" (3:21); "Slaves, obey your earthly masters" (3:22); and "Masters, treat your slaves with justice and fairness" (4:1). What is so striking about this is that the same results occur from being "filled by the Spirit" as do from "let[ting] the word of Christ dwell in you richly."

What do we conclude? Just this: Yielding to the authority of the Word of God in dealing with life's issues is the way our lives are lived under the influence and control of the Holy Spirit. In other words, having a biblical worldview and living under that biblical worldview is to live under the influence of the Holy Spirit. That is what the Holy Spirit uses to influence our thinking so as to produce the godly living. Further, it has to do with our momentary choices; it is not a state of being that we enter.

62

Related to this, of course, is the directive of Romans 12:2, "Do not be conformed to this present world, but be transformed by the renewing of your mind, so that you may test and approve what is the will of God – what is good and well-pleasing and perfect."

As we learn God's word and live obediently to it – making our evaluations about life and yielding to its authority in making our decisions – we live under the influence of the Holy Spirit. It makes sense, then, that if a Christian does not know God's word, either because he is a babe or has persisted in being a babe, he cannot think and live biblically – and therefore cannot live consistently under the influence of the Holy Spirit. And recall what we said earlier: a baby is characteristically fleshly; his core beliefs are based on something other than the word of God.

The spiritual person is the mature person who consistently and characteristically lives his life under the influence of the Holy Spirit through God's word. The results of that lifestyle are seen in his godly behavior (see Eph. 5:18-21) and the fruit of the Spirit that is lived out in his life (see Gal. 5:22-23). It is in this state of maturity that this person can be said to be "filled up to all the fullness of God" (see Eph. 3:19).

7

Qualified to Inherit

The preacher was nearly in tears as he described the plight of a young boy who had become orphaned at age twelve and had lived on the streets for the next two years. His parents had been killed in an automobile accident and there were no relatives to care for him. Initially, he had been placed in a foster home but, in anger over the loss of his parents, he had run away.

Living on the street had been difficult, particularly as a child. Adults could defend themselves and the police left them alone. But for a young boy, it was a different story. He was constantly on the lookout for troublemakers, and often he had to play "hide and seek" with the police.

Meals consisted mostly of what he would glean from the trash cans of nearby restaurants.

It was on a real cool evening in October, that he decided to sleep under a pile of cardboard boxes that had been discarded in the alley next to his "favorite restaurant." He hadn't been asleep long when he was awakened by the sound of a car door slamming and several voices.

"I wonder how he got here?" he heard one of them say. "Looks like a runaway to me," came the reply. Suddenly, he felt a big hand on his shoulder. "Wake up, son," the voice said. In an instant his eyes were as large as silver dollars. As he drew himself to his feet, there, before him were three men – one of whom was very well dressed, and obviously in charge of the other two.

"Why are you out here in the cold?" the well-dressed man asked. "Don't you have a home?" He could tell they were not the police. But who were they? "What do ya want to know for?" he shot back. "As we were driving past the alley, I noticed you lying among those boxes and I was concerned that you might be hurt."

"No one cares about me," the boy said. "That's not true, I care," said the man. "Are you going to call the police?" asked the boy. "Have you done something wrong?" came the reply. "No!" exclaimed the boy. "Then come on and get into the car. I'll take you to my home. You can get something to eat and then get some rest.

Somewhat reluctantly, he climbed into the car. Within a few minutes, the car turned into an entrance that was flanked by big iron gates. A guard house soon appeared as they made they way down a long, winding driveway.

"I've never seen such a house," the boy thought to himself as they pulled up in front of the house. The inside of the house was even more breathtaking. There were many large rooms, and a huge winding stairway leading to the second floor. "He must be a very rich man; I wonder who he is?"

By this time, the preacher had everyone's attention. He went on to explain how the man built a relationship with the boy and actually adopted him as his own son and made him his heir. That, the preacher continued to explain, is exactly what God did for us – He adopted us into His family, and we are now His children.

An interesting, emotionally charged story, but his application was totally inaccurate!

Ephesians 1:5 says that God "predestined us to adoption as his sons through Jesus Christ, according to the pleasure of his will." And like the preacher in our story, many have wrongly taught or have been taught that as a

66

result of believing in Christ, one becomes a member of God's family by adoption.

We become a child of God by birth, not by adoption. The notion of "adoption as his sons" is vitally important, but we must be careful to distinguish it from "being born again."

Born of God

Unlike the young boy in the story, the condition of the unbeliever, the natural man, is much worse. He is, in fact, dead! The Apostle Paul explains his condition like this: "And although you were dead in your transgressions and sins, in which you formerly lived according to this world's present path, according to the ruler of the kingdom of the air, the ruler of the spirit that is now energizing the sons of disobedience, among whom all of us also formerly lived out our lives in the cravings of our flesh, indulging the desires of the flesh and the mind, and were by nature children of wrath even as the rest" (Eph. 2:1-3).

In that condition, there is "no one who seeks God" (Rom. 3:11); their mind is "hostile to God, for it does not submit to the law of God, nor is it able to do so" (Rom. 8:7).

Keep in mind that the natural man has the ability to believe or trust. This is human volition. It is an attribute of man. In fact, all people really live "by faith." Whatever one follows as a philosophy of life or worldview becomes the basis of one's thoughts and actions. Therefore, life is lived on the basis of what one actually believes in or trusts.

The fundamental problem, however, is that the nature of the unbeliever is biased toward self and away from God. Being spiritually dead, he "does not receive the things of the Spirit of God, for they are foolishness to him.

And he cannot understand them, because they are spiritually discerned" (1 Cor. 2:14).

By nature, the unbeliever man of himself not only will not, but cannot believe in the gospel of Jesus Christ,. Not having an ability to understand the wisdom of God, the gospel to him is "foolishness" (1 Cor. 1:18). That is why Jesus said, "No one can come to me unless the Father who sent me draws him" (Jn. 6:44). However, He does add that "everyone who hears and learns from the Father comes to me" (Jn. 6:45). But who are those who hear and learn from the Father?

Jesus Himself identified them as "My sheep" (Jn. 10:1-30). He knows them and they know Him (v. 14). He lays down His life for them (v. 15). Those who are not His sheep do not believe in Him *because* they are not His sheep (v. 26). Those who are His sheep will believe in Him (v. 27); He gives eternal life to them (v. 28a); and they shall never perish (v. 28b).

Paul describes those same people as those chosen by God "before the foundation of the world" (Eph. 1:3); as those "foreknown" by God (Rom. 8:29); and as those uniquely formed by God as "objects of mercy that he prepared beforehand for glory" (Rom. 9:23).

It is true the unbeliever must believe in Christ to be saved (Acts 15:31). It is equally true that he cannot. The important question therefore is this: How, then, will anyone ever be saved?

The answer is, very simply, by the grace of God. One is not saved by faith, but by grace. Faith is the "pipe" through which it flows.

Because of man's lost condition, his salvation is totally the work of God [cf. 1 Cor. 1:30a; Eph. 2:5,8 ("have been saved" is in the Greek perfect tense – completed action in past time with continuing results, and is in the passive voice); see also 1 Pet. 1:3], but the process does follow logical order.

The whole process happens at the same moment, but because several things happen at that moment, a logical sequence is formed. 1 John 5:1 states that "everyone who believes that Jesus is the Christ (present tense) has been fathered by God" (perfect tense). In grammatical sequence, the begetting precedes the believing.

It is amazing that a natural man can actually become born of God! This is what Jesus explained to Nicodemus in John 3, "Unless one is born from above he cannot see the kingdom of God" (v. 3).

Several clear examples of this process are presented in Scripture. In 2 Thessalonians 2:13, Paul writes, "But we ought to give thanks for you always, brothers and sisters, loved by the Lord, because God chose you from the beginning for salvation through sanctification by the Spirit and faith in the truth. He called you to this salvation through our gospel, so that you may possess the glory of our Lord Jesus Christ."

In Acts 16:14, we are given the account of the first person to come to Christ in Europe. "A woman named Lydia, a dealer in purple cloth from the city of Thyatira, a God-fearing woman, listening to us. The Lord opened her heart to respond to what Paul was saying."

The process seems clear enough: those who have been chosen by the Father before the foundation of the world are those foreknown by Him, and they are those who are the sheep of the Lord Jesus Christ. The Lord Jesus Christ laid down His life for the sheep. He died in their place (cf. Matt. 20:28; Jn. 10:15; Rom. 5:8; 1 Pet. 1:17-18; et al). His death satisfied the justice of God for their sins (cf. Rom. 4:25). In a word, their salvation was totally and completely accomplished at the cross.

But the application of their salvation comes in time. Remember, we are speaking about logical sequence. At the point of regeneration by the Holy Spirit, an individual is made alive. As a "new creation" (2 Cor. 5:17), this one has the ability to believe or trust (thus making faith a gift of God's grace as well; cf. 2 Thess. 3:2; Phil. 1:29). Unlike his old nature that was biased away from God and toward self, his new nature is biased toward God. In this new created state, the gospel is no longer "foolishness" to him – it is now compelling (he is "called" through it; cf. 2 Thess. 2:14). He believes it, trusts in it. And his act of believing becomes the evidence of his regeneration (cf. Jn. 6:29; 1 Cor. 12:3). It is his first work of faith! He is now a child of God – by birth!

But, you may be asking yourself, what about all those passages that talk about being adopted? What is that all about?

Adoption as Sons

Even with all its inaccuracies about how we become a part of God's family, our opening story does have an element of truth to it. We *have been* "adopted as sons with full rights" (cf. Gal. 4:5). But as we have seen, "adoption" is not the way we became part of the family – that is by birth. Adoption has to do with rights and privileges as an heir in the family. The term adoption is found only in the New Testament (Rom. 8:15, 23; 9:4; Gal. 4:5; Eph. 1:5), where it is developed into a theological concept – and then, only by Paul. There are two principle points to be made: 1. Adoption stresses the release from slavery, where the former slave is granted all the rights and privileges as a son in the family; and, 2. Adoption is used to stress the legal rights of the heir – that as a son, one is fully qualified to share in the inheritance of the father.

70

It is with the second principle that we are primarily concerned in this study. In Christ, God has fully qualified each of His children as an heir.

In Colossians 1:10-14, the apostle relates how a worthy walk with God manifests itself. Verse 12 states, "giving thanks to the Father who has qualified you to share in the saints' inheritance in light." The reason for this thankfulness is given in verse 13, "For he delivered us from the power of darkness and transferred us to the kingdom of the Son he loves."

The phrase "who has qualified" is a translation of a Greek participle formed from the term *hikanoō*, which means "to make sufficient, to render fit." At the point of our regeneration – when we were transferred from the kingdom of darkness into the kingdom of the Son, we were rendered fit by the Father as an heir.

The Heir and the Inheritance

As we shall see in the next chapter, being qualified as an heir does not mean that every heir receives an equal share in the inheritance. The fact that an inheritance awaits us is well established. Peter tells us that our salvation from sin is with a view to "an inheritance, imperishable, undefiled, and unfading. It is reserved in heaven for you" (1 Pet. 1:4).

But there is also the matter of works of faith, a subject that we have fully developed in the ongoing chapters of this book. There is a direct relationship between our works of faith and our share in the inheritance in Christ.

To lay hold of all that is potentially ours in the inheritance, we must flesh out the truth of God's Word in the momentary situations and circumstances of life. Paul had this in mind when he addressed the elders from Ephesus: "And now entrust you to God and to the message of his grace. This message is able to build you up and give you an inheritance among all those who are sanctified" (Acts 20:32).

In his exhortation to the church at Colosse, he said, "Whatever you are doing, work at it with enthusiasm, as to the Lord and not for people, because you know that you will receive your inheritance from the Lord as the reward." (Col. 3:23-24).

Today, some of the things in our culture provide us with interesting illustrations. I remember well the wise counsel of a former theology professor. He would often remind his students not to push illustrations too far, for at some point, they all break down. With that in mind, let's use a cultural situation to illustrate the relationship between salvation and inheritance.

Many professional athletes have what is termed a "no-cut contract with incentive clauses." Basically, it means that they have a secure position on the team – they cannot be cut. As a member of the team, there are many things that he will share in common with the other players, simply because he is a member of the team. On the other hand, he has the opportunity to greatly increase his compensation through his performance. If he performs well, his compensation will be commensurate with his performance. If his performance is sub-standard, he will forfeit what could have been his.

The parallel is obvious. At the point of regeneration – when we trust in Christ as our sin bearer – we are justified by God in a forensic sense whereby He declares us righteous and treats us as such. By His power, we are kept in that state (cf. Jn. 10:27-30; 1 Pet. 1:5; 2 Tim. 2:13). As His children, we share many things in common, e.g. eternal life (Jn. 3:16); the righteousness of Christ (Rom. 3:22); a resurrection body (2 Cor. 15:50-58); the hope of heaven (Jn. 14:2,3; 2 Cor. 5:8); as well as many other things.

But there are things that are not shared in common – specifically, rewards and inheritance. These actually become "incentive clauses." How well are you doing? In the next chapter, we will look into the future to our final examination. Hopefully, it will spur us to action!

8
Our Final Examination

The afternoon sun was very hot, but I had hardly noticed. It was one of those rare moments of a lifetime. Sweat was rolling down my face and my heart was beating rapidly. I stood and watched as several dozen people walked ahead of me, pointing out different things that caught their eye. It was an incredible experience. I was standing in the main area of the Corinthian agora!

I had learned as a seminary student that every major city in ancient Greece had an agora (the Greek term for *marketplace*). It was very much like an open-air shopping mall. This one was L-shaped with shops lining both sides of the walkway. Temples for Grecian gods were there. There was a meat market, too, where one could buy fresh meat that had been used in sacrifices to the Grecian gods. Even the tent making shop of Aquila and his wife, Priscilla, had been located there.

As I looked around, I tried to visualize the slave trade that had been conducted there. Many human beings had been bought and sold in the Corinthian agora! I was also well aware that it was here where Paul had his day in court.

On his second missionary journey, Paul had been able to plant a Christian church in Corinth (Acts 18:1-17). In that day, Corinth was the metropolis of the Peloponnesus. It was strategically located on a narrow isthmus between the Aegean Sea and the Adriatic Sea that connects the Peloponnesus with northern Greece.

Corinth was a very religious city, being filled with shrines and temples, the most prominent being the Temple of Aphrodite which was situated atop an 1,800-foot promontory called the Acrocorinthus. Worshippers took full advantage of the 1,500 Hieroduli (temple prostitutes) as they worshipped the "goddess of love."

The city thrived on commerce, entertainment, immorality and corruption, and was notorious as a place of wealth and indulgence. "To live as a Corinthian" meant to live in luxury and immorality. It was into this environment our Lord had sent Paul to plant His church.

When Paul came into a new city, it was his custom to go first to the Jewish synagogue, because it was there he could present Christ as Messiah and show how He had fulfilled the promises of the Law and Prophets. And in the process, God was pleased to save some of them.

But those of the Jews who did not believe reacted violently toward Paul. Acts 18 records how they took Paul before Gallio, the proconsul of Achaia, charging that "this man is persuading people to worship God in a way contrary to the law!" (v. 13). Interestingly, the case was heard by Gallio at "the judgment seat" (vv. 12, 16).

As I turned to look behind me, I noticed what appeared to be a stage or platform. It was about four to five feet high, and its floor area was about the size of the family room in our house in Texas. It was framed by a stone wall, and my eye immediately fixed on a Greek inscription carved into one of the stones: *bēma* – the Greek term for "judgment seat." This was it, the judgment seat! The Corinthian church knew the *bēma* well.

The Corinthian church has been characterized in this way: though gifted and growing, the church was plagued with problems – moral and ethical, doctrinal and practical, corporate and private. One of their problems was that

76

they were taking each other to court over issues that should have been resolved in the church. Paul addresses the problem in 1 Cor. 6:1-8. But the point we are making is this: their litigation would have been addressed at the *bēma* located in the agora at Corinth!

A Picture Is Worth a Thousand Words

Modern research demonstrates that people have different styles of learning. Some are more analytical, others more conceptual, while still others require visualization. Not that a person learns totally one way or the other, it's just that individuals tend to be dominated more by one particular style.

These observations are particularly helpful to those of us who are teachers. To help people learn, we must communicate not only with words, but also with "pictures" – including verbal pictures.

Some 2,400 years ago, Solomon, King of Israel, said, "There is nothing truly new on earth. Is there anything about which someone can say, 'Look at this! It is new!'?" (Ecc. 1:9-10).

God knew about the "wordless book" even before its value was discovered. He also knew pictures, even verbal pictures, were a terrific aid to learning. He taught the children of Israel through "pictures" (cf. 1 Cor. 10:3-4). Jesus used "verbal pictures" (parables) to teach His disciples (cf. Matt. 13:10-17).

The Apostle Paul also used "verbal pictures." True, he demonstrates a clear, logical style in his writing, for the most part conceptualizing truth. But he also makes good use of the culture and experiences of his audience to facilitate learning.

For example, the Christians in Corinth had observed, indeed many had taken part in, the buying and selling of slaves in the agora. To help them understand the doctrine of redemption and its attendant consequences, Paul selected the Greek term *agorazō*, which means *to purchase in the market place*. Here is how he put it, "Or do you not know that your body is the temple of the Holy Spirit who is in you, whom you have from God, and that you are not your own? For you *were bought (agorazō)* with a price. Therefore glorify God with your body" (1 Cor. 6:19-20).

God had purchased them out of the "slave market" of sin, and they now belong to Him.

In his second letter to that same church, Paul carefully explained that the manner in which they conducted their lives was of critical importance. Everything you do, he said, should be done with the "ambition to please him" (2 Cor. 5:9). But why? "For we must all appear before the judgment seat (*bēma*) of Christ, so that each one may be paid back according to what he has done while in the body, whether good or evil" (v. 10).

Paul had said something about works and their value in his first letter (cf. 1 Cor. 3:10-15). But he hadn't used the term *bēma*. Now they really have a clear picture of what it is all about. Some day, every believer will have to stand before the judge – not Gallio, but the Lord Jesus Christ – and give an account of himself!

The Judgment Seat of Christ

Standing in front of the *bēma* in Corinth made a big impression on me. I could visualize myself standing in that public place and the Lord Jesus Christ standing in the seat of judgment. If I listened carefully, I could almost hear my name called.

"I wonder what I will receive," I thought to myself. I tried to run through the years of my life in a moment of time. The thousands upon thousands of thoughts that I

78

had entertained in my mind, the words that I had spoken, the actions I had performed – of what value were they, really?

Recall from earlier chapters that our soul-life is composed of our thoughts, words and actions. Recall also that the Scripture states that these very components will be subjected to judgment (cf. 1 Cor. 4:5; Matt. 12:36; Eph. 6:8). Some of our thoughts, words and actions have been expressed on the basis of faith. These are what the Bible calls "good works" (Eph. 2:10) and "proven faith" (1 Pet. 1:7). Everything else is referred to as "dead works" (Heb. 6:1; 9:14). Dead works, of course, are those that, before God, are useless and have no value.

At the judgment seat of Christ, the issue is not justification. That was accomplished at the cross and applied to every believer in regeneration. The issue is rewards and inheritance. What rewards and inheritance are will be addressed in the next chapter. The subject of our current consideration is the relationship of rewards and inheritance to our soul-life and the judgment seat of Christ.

Paul says that each Believer will be "paid back according to what he has done." Earlier in this book, we pointed out that the term recompense (Gr. *komizō*) means to receive back something that is due, or to get for one's self by earning.

Are we to understand that we actually earn something from God? Precisely! "But," someone will protest, "the Bible says that we are saved by grace through faith, and 'not as a result of works, that no one should boast'" (cf. Eph. 2:8-9). That is exactly our point. Although directly related to and growing out of justification, sanctification is distinct from it. The terms for sanctification are quite different from those of justification, and one makes an extremely serious error if that distinction is not acknowledged. If such acknowledgement is not made, the gospel of Christ becomes faith *plus* "works." Believe in Christ *plus* "Be baptized." Believe in Christ *plus* "Walk down the aisle." Believe in Christ *plus* "Make Him Lord of your life." The list is endless.

When a person trusts in Christ for the forgiveness of sins and eternal life, he is believing in one who *is* Lord! Whether or not he lives under the Lordship of Christ experientially is a different matter, as the example of the Corinthian church attests.

At the judgment seat of Christ, our works of faith actually earn rewards and inheritance. Remember the illustration of the professional athlete's no-cut contract with incentive clauses we discussed in the last chapter? When we are born of God – regenerated – we become a "member of the team." At that point, certain things become ours automatically: justification, the indwelling of the Holy Spirit, a new body, heaven, etc. But most aspects of the inheritance in Christ, including rewards, are the "incentive clauses."

"Incentive clause" accomplishments require commitment and choice. That is why we observe so many appeals to volition in the Scriptures. The imperative mood in New Testament Greek is used for this purpose. It is true that an imperative statement expresses a command. But the more fundamental intent of the imperative mood is to express appeal to volition. In fact, in New Testament Greek, it is the strongest way to make an appeal to volition.

"Make every effort to present yourself before God as a proven worker who does not need to be ashamed, teaching the message of truth accurately" (2 Tim. 2:15). "I, therefore, the prisoner of the Lord, urge you to live worthily of the calling with which you have been called"

(Eph. 4:1). "Continue working out your salvation with awe and reverence" (Phil. 2:12). "Whatever you are doing, work at it with enthusiasm, as to the Lord and not for people, because you know that you will receive your inheritance from the Lord as the reward. Serve the Lord Christ" (Col. 3:23-24). "For you were called to freedom, brothers and sisters, only do not use your freedom as an opportunity to indulge your flesh, but through love serve one another" (Gal. 5:13).

These verses are examples of appeal to volition. To obey them expresses faith and commitment. Sometimes we obey, sometimes we don't. That's why at the judgment seat of Christ, judgment will be rendered "according to what he has done while in the body, whether good or evil" (2 Cor. 5:10).

Tested By Fire

One can only imagine the scene in the agora's jewelry store – people milling around the displays of gold, silver and precious stones. In the corner of the shop, they could watch as ore was being placed in a large crucible and then heated until it reached a liquid state. When the ore reached that point, the dross – the worthless part – was skimmed off, leaving the pure gold to be used for jewelry.

The process presented an interesting contrast. The fire had an opposite effect on two of the elements involved: it burned up the wood used to heat the crucible, and it purified and made more valuable the precious metal contained in the crucible. No doubt, Paul had observed this scene on many occasions. "Our works are just like that," he must have thought.

To make clear the relationship between works of faith, rewards, inheritance, and the judgment seat of Christ, he combined two aspects of the agora – the jewelry store and the judgment seat.

81

In 1 Corinthians 3:12-15, he sets it all out. Our works – thoughts, words, actions – are likened to "gold, silver, precious stones, wood hay, straw: (v. 12). Obviously, the gold, silver and precious stones represent our *good works* (proven faith). The wood, hay and straw represent our *dead works*.

In that day (the judgment seat of Christ), the quality of our work will become evident, "because it will be revealed by fire" (v. 13a). Our soul-life is the sum total of our works – good works, dead works. The issue, therefore, is quality or value, and Paul adds "the fire will test what kind of work each has done" (v. 13b; see also 1 Pet. 1:7).

For the term *test*, both writers chose the Greek word *dokimazō*. This is important. The judgment seat of Christ is not with a view to condemnation. That issue was settled at the cross. The fact is clearly stated in Romans 8:1, "There is therefore now no condemnation for those who are in Christ Jesus." And the New Covenant adds, "And their sins and their lawless deeds I will remember no longer" (Heb. 10:17).

Dokimazō means to put something to the test, to examine something, with the thought of giving approval to it.

A young lady in our church once told me the story of how she had been walking in the local mall and noticed a sign in the window of a jewelry store that read, "Free Appraisals." She had recently been given a diamond engagement ring and wondered about its value. When she went into the store, the jeweler took the ring, put a glass magnifier in his eye, and examined (*dokimazō*) the stone. The examination was not for the purpose of condemning the stone – although the same examination could have certainly proven it to be of no value, had that been the case. Fortunately for her, the stone was proven to be valuable!

When our Lord evaluates our works, the fire of Paul's illustration represents the test. Perhaps this is what John the Baptist had in mind when he said, "I baptize you with water, but one more powerful than I is coming – I am not worthy to untie the strap of his sandals. He will baptize you with the Holy Spirit and fire" (Lk. 3:16). Jesus Christ baptizes us with the Holy Spirit at the beginning (the point of regeneration, cf. Acts 11:15-16) and baptizes us with fire at his judgment seat.

Well, here we are – at the judgment seat of Christ. Our works are before us, and the Savior has a torch in His hand. What will be the outcome? "If what someone has built survives," Paul said, "he will receive a reward" (v. 14).

My own accumulation of works is soon hidden from view by the smoke as the "wood, hay and straw" is quickly consumed. It is quite a shock to watch, as it appears my life is literally "going up in smoke!"

Soon, the smoke clears. The pile, certainly a lot smaller than it was, is, thank God, not a total loss!

I'm constrained to think what could have been mine if only I had chosen to more completely "lose my life for Christ's sake." Paul had warned me. "If someone's work is burned up, he will suffer loss." It's obvious to me now that the loss he had in mind was all that might have been mine. My actual rewards are based on what is left, what has abiding value, what remains as proof of my faith – the "gold, silver and precious stones."

Looking back on my life, it is all now so clear. My soul-life, represented by my thoughts, words and actions, has actually been exchanged for a share in the rewards and inheritance associated with obedience to Christ. In that sense, I have saved or delivered my soul-life into eternity. As Peter put it, "attaining the goal of your faith – the salvation of your souls" (1 Pet. 1:9).

But what exactly are my rewards and inheritance? What is it that awaits me at the end of the "race of life?" To this subject we now turn out attention.

9

Our Inheritance in Christ

What a magnificent thought! As believers in Christ, we are the appointed heirs to the kingdom of God!

Like you, I have heard of people inheriting large fortunes, but that kind of thing is so foreign to my experience, it is difficult to really grasp what it means. In all likelihood, most people feel the same way. At best, it can be little more than a dream.

The same thing is true when we talk about our being an heir of God. What does it mean? What will we inherit? Are there any conditions to be met? These are only a few of the many questions that might be asked. But as we come to the end of this book, what better subject could we address than what will be ours – or might have been ours – in life everlasting.

An Important Warning

In 1 Corinthians 6:9-10 and Ephesians 5:5, the Apostle Paul makes the strong assertion that certain people will not inherit the kingdom of God! Listen to what he says: "For you can be confident of this one thing, that no person who is immoral, impure, or greedy (such a person is an idolater) has any inheritance in the kingdom of Christ and God" (Eph. 5:5). "Do you not know that the unrighteous will not inherit the kingdom of God? Do not be deceived! The sexually immoral, idolaters, adulterers, passive homosexual partners, practicing, thieves, the greedy, drunkards, the verbally abusive, and swindlers will not inherit the kingdom of God" (1 Cor. 6:9-10).

Some have taken the phrase "kingdom of God" to refer to heaven and teach that if a person who claims to be a Christian commits any of these sins, it means that he loses his salvation and will not go to heaven. Others say if a person who claims to be a Christian "practices" such sins, it indicates that he was not really saved at all (recognizing that once a person is saved he cannot be lost again). But are these views supported by either context? The answer is a clear NO!

In 1 Corinthians 6, Paul is contrasting unbelievers with believers to exhort believers to godly living. In verse 11, he states, "Some of you once lived this way. But you were washed, you were sanctified, you were justified in the name of the Lord Jesus Christ and by the Spirit of our God."

The Corinthians were living very much like unbelievers. In fact, Paul asks them, "Are you not influenced by the flesh and behaving like unregenerate people?" (1 Cor. 3:3). What did he have in mind? Just this: when they were saved, they were characteristically fleshly because they were infants – they didn't know any better; but now, five years later, they are still controlled by their flesh. Why? They had refused to grow! (cf. 1 Cor. 3:1-2). They had had very good teaching (Paul, Apollos, Peter), but they had not lived out what they had been taught. As a result, spiritually, they had grown very little – if at all!

In chapter six, he warns them about the consequences of living by the flesh – which is the opposite of living by the Spirit by faith. His argument is essentially this: since unbelievers do not inherit the kingdom of God, why should you want to live like them? To do so is totally unprofitable, and the implication is that you forfeit your inheritance in the kingdom to the extent you choose to live like them!

Clearly, Paul is not saying they forfeit heaven – regeneration took them from being *one of them* to being what they are, children of God. He is saying they forfeit some aspects of the inheritance that might have been theirs! The context of the Ephesians passage teaches the same thing.

From what we have developed in earlier chapters of this book and what we have just presented, I hope God has your attention. If we do not live to please God – living by faith within the parameters of His word – we forfeit our inheritance with Christ! That makes life a serious business, doesn't it!

A Review of Some Basics

As believers in Christ, we have been born into God's family (1 Jn. 5:1), and He has thereby qualified us as His heirs (Rom. 8:17; Col. 1:12). Thus, the inheritance is established now and will be realized in the future (1 Pet. 1:4). Some aspects of the inheritance are shared by all believers: justification (Rom. 5:1), the unconditional righteousness of Christ (Rom. 3:22), reconciliation (Rom. 5:11), heaven (Jn. 14:2-3), a resurrection body (1 Cor. 15:50-58), et al.

However, some aspects of the inheritance are conditional. Listen to the Scripture: "And now I entrust you to God and to the message of his grace. This message is able to build you up and give you an inheritance among all those who are sanctified" (Acts 20:32).

Paul is saying these words to the elders of the church at Ephesus. The emphasis of the statement is on their relationship to God's word. Lived out in life, it is able to do two things: 1. Build them up in maturity; and 2. Give them an inheritance in Christ. Clearly, the reverse is true. If they do not live out God's word in life, they will not mature spiritually and will, in the end, forfeit the inheritance that could have been theirs!

Because most Christians don't like to think about "earning" anything from God, they react emotionally against any view of sanctification that speaks of works. But God tells us that we were "created in Christ Jesus for good works that God prepared beforehand so we may do them" (Eph. 2:10). And we should also understand that our works of faith actually earn inheritance: "Whatever you are doing, work at it with enthusiasm, as to the Lord, and not for people, because you know that you will receive your inheritance from the Lord as your reward" (Col. 3:23-24).

Gaining a Clear Perspective

As we think in terms of putting some definition to the various aspects of the inheritance, we need to be sure we have the big picture in mind. Let me explain.

When God created the first man, Adam, he gave him (and the human race that existed in Adam) a commission: mankind was to rule over the earth. The scope of that rule was stated in this way: "... so they my rule over the fish of the sea and the birds of the air, over the cattle, and over all the earth, and over all the creatures that move on the earth" (Gen. 1:26). He was to subdue it and rule over it (Gen. 1:28). But because of Adam's sin, we do not see man ruling over the earth in this way. However, the thought of man one day ruling over the earth passed from generation to generation.

Having been in Israel and having walked in the areas around Bethlehem where the shepherds tended their sheep, in my mind's eye I can picture David sitting on a hillside one evening looking up into the heavens. The sky is clear and the stars seem to number in the millions. The moon is shining brightly. He later records his thoughts of that moment:

"When I look up at the heavens, which your fingers made, and see the moon and the stars, which you set in place, I think, 'Of what importance is the human race, that you should notice them? Of what importance is mankind, that you should pay attention to them, and make them almost like the heavenly beings?' You grant mankind honor and majesty; you allow them to rule over your creation; you have placed everything under their authority, including all the sheep and cattle, as well as the wild animals, the birds in the sky, the fish in the sea and everything that moves through the channels of the seas. O Lord, our sovereign Master, how magnificent is your reputation throughout the earth!" (Ps. 8:3-9).

David clearly understood the commission that God had given to mankind. But he didn't understand any more than Adam. He saw the rule of man as being over sheep and cattle, wild animals, birds in the sky, and the fish in the sea. Is that it? Is there more? And when and how will it take place?

We must keep in mind the progressive nature of God's revelation. It would not be until the first century A.D. that God would supply the answers to these questions. We find them in part in the letter to the Hebrews. In the first chapter, the writer tells us that God has appointed the Lord Jesus Christ "heir of all things" (v. 2). He has given him the name "Son" in the sense of "firstborn and heir." As such, He will rule over all creation. Every creature will bow before Him. Paul put it this way: "God exalted him and gave him the name that is above every name, so that at the name of Jesus every knee will bow – in heaven and on earth and under the earth – and every tongue confess that Jesus Christ is Lord to the glory of God the Father" (Phil. 2:9-11).

The Lord Jesus Christ is the last Adam – the Adam of Genesis being the first (1 Cor. 15:45). In the first Adam, all die. But in the last Adam, Christ, all shall be made alive (1 Cor. 15:22). In other words, there are two human races: one which is made up of every human being that is born into this world, and the other made up of human beings who have been born of the Spirit of God. Those of the second human race are referred to as the "sons of God" (Rom. 8:14), and the "brothers and sisters" of the Lord Jesus Christ (Rom. 8:29). Jesus actually refers to those who believe in Him as his "brothers and sisters" (Heb. 2:11-12).

Now think about the commission to "man." Could it be that God had the second human race in mind the whole time? Let's take a look.

In Hebrews 2, the writer states that God "did not put the world to come ... under the control of angels" (v. 5). But notice the passage he quotes to state who will rule over the world to come: "What is man that you think of him or the son of man that you care for him? You made him lower than the angels for a little while. You crowned him with glory and honor. You put all things under his control" (vv. 6-8).

It is interesting that the writer stops short of the application that David saw – animals, birds and fish. He ends with, "You put *all things* under his control" emphasis mine). Now look at his application: "For when he put all things under his control, he left nothing outside of his control. At the present time we do not yet see all things under his control, but we see Jesus, who was made lower than the angels for a little while, now crowned with glory and honor" (vv. 8-9).

The commission to "man" finds its fulfillment in the Lord Jesus Christ! He is Heir of all things! The inheritance of God is for the Son and his brothers and sisters. But there is a subtle aspect to this that is seldom pointed out, and we need to consider it carefully.

In God's sovereign plan for the ages, He has decreed everything that will ever come to pass. However, it is important also to remember that not only has He decreed the ends of all things, but also the *means* to those ends. Let's apply this principle to the issue at hand.

In eternity past, God decreed that man (the human race) would ultimately rule over His creation. And the human race He had in mind was the second human race headed by the Lord Jesus Christ. But how could this be done? Through the incarnation!

John 1 tells us that the Word, Who was with God and was God, "became flesh and took up residence among us. We saw his glory – the glory of the one and only, full of grace and truth, who came from the Father" (v. 14). Being born of a woman, He gained His humanity, thus becoming the God-Man – fully God and fully man, united in one person forever.

Anticipating His ultimate fulfillment of the commission given to "man," Christ Jesus mostly referred to Himself as "Son of Man" (cf. Matt. 8:20; 9:6; 10:23; 11:19; 12:8, 32, 40; 13:37, 41; et al).

In this book, we have argued that our inheritance in Christ is based on works of faith. If you are still wrestling with the concept, I trust that what follows will dispel all doubt. Remember the principle of "means to the end"? Consider this: our Lord gained *His* inheritance through His obedience to the Father! Thus, He becomes an example for us! Listen to His prayer in John 17:

91

"Father, the time has come. Glorify your Son, so that your Son may glorify you – just you have given him authority over all humanity, so that he may give eternal life to everyone you have given him. Now this is eternal life – that they know you, the only true God, and Jesus Christ, whom you sent. Glorified you on the earth by completing the work you gave me to do. And now, Father, glorify me at your side with the glory I had with you before the world was created" (vv. 1-5).

Now put this together with what Paul writes in Philippians 2:

"You should have the same attitude toward one another that Christ Jesus had, who though he existed in the form of God did not regard equality with God as something to be grasped, but emptied himself by taking on the form of a slave, by looking like other men, and by sharing in human nature. He humbled himself, by becoming obedient to the point of death – even death on a cross! As a result God exalted him and gave him the name that is above every name, so that at the name of Jesus, every knee will bow – in heaven and on earth and under the earth – and every tongue confess that Jesus is Lord to the glory of God the Father" (vv. 5-11).

Don't miss the point: the exaltation of the Son came as a consequence of His obedience! And as the First-born of the second human race, it is *His* inheritance that we share!

One final point before we move on. In Romans 8, Paul addresses the subject of our being "children of God" (v. 16). As children of God, we are qualified as heirs – having received the "Spirit of adoption" (v. 15). Consequently, we are *all* "heirs of God" (v. 17). This refers to the portion of the inheritance we share in common because we are "children of God." But the first-born is a double-portion heir (an historically established fact). To share in the blessings of the first-born requires commitment and obedience. Listen to what Paul says: "And if children, then heirs (namely, heirs of God and also fellow-heirs with Christ) – if indeed we suffer with him so we may also be glorified with Him" (v. 17). In other words, if we are going to share in Christ's inheritance, we must enter into His sufferings through obedient, faithful living in the light of God's Word.

The Inheritance of Christ

Since we know that *our* inheritance is related to *Christ's* inheritance, let's look at His first.

Our Lord's rule is over all creation, i.e. "all things" (Heb. 2:8). Some of it is expressed temporally – as Israel's King. His rule is "over the house of Jacob" (Lk. 1:33); and "over the gentiles" (Rom. 15:12).

The temporal expression of the kingdom will be for "a thousand years" (Rev. 20:6); and He will reign "until he has put all his enemies under his feet" (1 Cor. 15:25). Moving on from the temporal, His kingdom is said to be "forever and ever" (Rev. 11:15).

The Old Testament tells us a great deal about the temporal expression of the kingdom. It is related primarily to the literal promises to Abraham and his seed. Yet we know very little about the eternal kingdom.

The Inheritance of Believers

One of the problems we face in dealing with our inheritance is that the Scriptures use very general terms to describe it. Even so, we can gain enough insight to be able to build a fairly clear picture of what it will be like. Some of the terms address the inheritance directly, while others,

93

like crowns and the promises to the conquerors in Revelation 2 and 3, seem to particularize the inheritance for certain individuals. The more general expressions include:

The earth. "Blessed are the meek, for they will inherit the earth" (Matt. 5:5).

Eternal life. "And everyone who has left houses or brothers or sisters or father or mother or children or fields for my sake will receive a hundred times as much and will inherit eternal life" (Matt. 19:29; cf. Mk. 10:17; Lk. 10:25; 18:18).

The kingdom. "Then the king will say to those on his right, 'Come, you who are blessed by my Father, inherit the kingdom prepared for you from the foundation of the world'" (Matt. 25:34).

An imperishable body. "Now this is what I am saying, brothers and sisters: Flesh and blood cannot inherit the kingdom of God, nor does the perishable inherit the imperishable" (1 Cor. 15:50).

Salvation. "Are they [angels] not all ministering spirits, sent out to serve those who will inherit salvation?" (Heb. 1:14).

The promises. "But we passionately want each of you to demonstrate the same eagerness for the fulfillment of your hope until the end, so that you may not be sluggish, but imitators of those who through faith and perseverance inherit the promises" (Heb. 6:11-12).

A blessing. "Finally, all of you be harmonious, sympathetic, affectionate, compassionate, and humble. Do not return evil for evil or insult for insult, but instead bless others because you were called to inherit a blessing" (1 Pet. 3:8-9).

When we look at the matter of *rewards*, the first thing we learn is that they will be received in heaven: "Blessed

94

are you when people insult you and persecute you and say all kinds of evil things against you falsely on account of me. Rejoice and be glad because your reward is great in heaven" (Matt. 5:11-12; cf. Matt. 16:12; Rev. 22:12).

"For if you love those who love you, what reward do you have? Even the tax collectors do the same, don't they?" (Matt. 5:46).

"For the Son of Man will come with his angels in the glory of His Father, and then he will reward each person according to what he has done" (Matt. 16:27).

"The one who plants and the one who waters work as one, but each will receive his reward according to his work" (1 Cor. 3:8).

"If what someone has built survives, he will receive a reward" (1 Cor. 3:14).

"Watch out, so that you do not lose what we have worked for, but receive a full reward" (2 Jn. 8).

The matter of *crowns* gets a lot more personal. A crown is a *symbol* of victory, honor, or distinction. Therefore, to crown someone is to confer upon them honor, dignity, or reward.

We need to realize that what we are naturally as unbelievers, and what Satan tries to get us as believers to do now is to seek the honor of men. It is a part of this world system. People will do unbelievable things for a plaque to go on their wall, a trophy to put on their mantle, etc. Did not the Lord warn us about this kind of motivation: "Be careful not to display your righteousness merely to be seen by people. Otherwise you have no reward with your Father in heaven. Thus whenever you do charitable giving, do not blow a trumpet before you, as the hypocrites do in the synagogues and on the streets so that people will praise them. I tell you the truth, they have their reward" (Matt. 6:1-2).

We need to think in eternal terms, not in temporal. That which is temporal will perish. Paul put it this way: "Do you not know that all the runners in a stadium compete, but only one receives the prize? So run to win. Each competitor must exercise self-control in everything. They do it to receive a perishable crown, but we an imperishable one" (1 Cor. 9:24-25).

Crowns can also be forfeited: "Hold on to what you have so that no one can take away your crown" (Rev. 3:11).

There are four crowns that are mentioned:

Crown of righteousness. "I have competed well; I have finished the race; I have kept the faith! Finally the crown of righteousness is reserved for me. The Lord, the righteous Judge, will award it to me in that day – and not to me only, but also to all who have set their affections on his appearing" (2 Tim. 4:7-8).

Crown of glory and honor. "You crowned him [man] with glory and honor" (Heb. 2:7; cf. 2:9).

Crown of life. "happy is the one who endures testing, because when he has proven to be genuine, he will receive the crown of life that God promised to those who love him" (Ja. 1:12; cf. Rev. 2:10).

Crown of glory. "So as your fellow elder and witness of Christ's sufferings and as one who shares in the glory that will be revealed, I urge the elders among you: Give a shepherd's care to God's flock among you, exercising oversight not merely as a duty but willingly under God's direction, not for shameful profit but eagerly. And do not lord it over those entrusted to you, but be examples to the flock. Then when the Chief Shepherd appears, you will receive the crown of glory that never fades away" (1 Pet. 5:1-4).

The final aspect regarding our inheritance has to do with the promises to the conquers. In 1 John 5:3-5, we are told that the love of God is to "that we keep his commandments" (v. 3a); and then John adds that "his commandments do not weigh us down" (v. 3b). Our love for God manifests itself in obedience to His word (cf. Jn. 14:14, 21, 23-24). When we live in obedience to His word, we are conquering the world, the flesh and the devil; the lust of the eyes, the lust of the flesh, and the sinful pride of life (cf. Rom 12:2; Gal. 5:16-17; Ja. 4:7; 1 Jn. 2:15-17).

For the sum of these, John uses the term "world," and he anticipates that all believers will, to some extent, be conquers (v. 4a). Indeed, because of faith in Christ as our Savior, we have "conquered" and are the only ones who can keep on conquering: "Now who is the person who has conquered the world except the one who believes that Jesus is the Son of God?" (v. 5).

When John came to write the Book of Revelation, The Lord Jesus Christ gave him promises to communicate to those who are conquerors. Relating this to our earlier study, all believers are conquerors in the sense of being saved from the penalty of sin. However, not all believers continue on as faithful conquerors!

To borrow an earlier illustration, when the nation of Israel left Egypt, it pictured our redemption in Christ. Their looking to their inheritance which God had set before them pictures our looking to our inheritance in Christ that is reserved in heaven for us. In essence, God told them, "Your inheritance (the land) is set before you – it is yours, but you must posses it. You must conquer those who are in the land. Do not intermarry with the them, do not make agreements with them – drive them out of the land and possess it. I have given you all the resources you need, and I will fight your battles for you."

Ironically, they never totally possessed the land. Why? Because of disobedience and unbelief. They forfeited what could have been theirs! And we can do the same thing. We forfeit aspects of our promised inheritance if we fail to be faithful conquerors.

The Promises to Conquerors

"To the one who conquers, I will permit him to eat from the tree of life that is in the paradise of God" (Rev. 2:7). What Adam lost we gain in Christ: "This is the bread that came down from heaven; it is not like the bread your ancestors ate, but then later died. The one who eats this bread will live forever" (Jn. 6:58).

"The one who conquers will in no way be harmed by the second death" (Rev. 2:11). Jesus said, "the one who lives and believes in me will never die" (Jn. 11:26).

"To the one who conquers, I will give him some of the hidden manna, and I will give him a white stone, and on that stone will be written a name that no one can understand except the one who receives it" (Rev. 2:17). This promise stresses the fact that there will be different levels of relationship with the Lord in heaven. Like John 14:21, it stresses intimacy and familiarity: "The person who has My commandments and obeys them is the one who loves me. The one who loves me will be loved by my Father, and I will love him and will reveal myself to him."

"The one who conquers and who continues in my deeds until the end, I will give him authority over the nations – he will rule them with an iron rod and like clay jars he will break them to pieces, just as I have received the right to rule from my Father – and I will give him the morning star" (Rev. 2:26-28). This involves reigning with Christ.

"The one who conquers will be dressed like them in white clothing, and I will never erase his name from the book of life, but will declare his name before my Father and before his angels" (Rev. 3:5). The theme of white garments is used in two ways: (1) to refer to our positional righteousness (Rev. 7:14); and (2) to our works of righteousness (Rev. 19:8). The second half of the statement is an affirmation of what our Lord said in John 10:27-28, "My sheep listen to my voice, and I know them, and they follow me. I give them eternal life, and they will never perish; no one will snatch them from my hand."

In the context of Matthew 10, our Lord taught His disciples about persecution and their active identification with Him. In verses 32 and 33 He said, "Whoever, then, acknowledges me before people, I will acknowledge before my Father in heaven. But whoever denies me before people, I will deny him before my Father in heaven." He ends the discourse by relating it to the possible loss of rewards (vv.40-42).

"The one who conquers I will make a pillar in the temple of my God, and he will never depart from it. I will write on him the name of my God and the name of the city of my God (the new Jerusalem that comes down out of heaven from my God), and my new name as well" (Rev. 3:12). This has to do with priestly privilege (cf. Zech. 3:1-10) and also stresses our identification with God. Every conqueror is both *with* God and *identified* with God.

"I will grant the one who conquers permission to sit with me on my throne, just as I too conquered and sat down with my Father on his throne" (Rev. 3:21). Those who overcome will reign with Christ in power and authority. This is not for every believer. Paul writes to Timothy that "If we endure, we will reign with Him" (2 Tim. 2:12a).

We certainly have not exhausted all that could be said about our inheritance. It is a vitally important subject, yet one sadly neglected. As we approach the coming of our Savior, the Spirit of God is moving to make these truths more widely known – and you can help! Spread the word! Share this book with your friends and loved ones. The time to spread the greatness of this message is now!

Remember the words of our Lord Jesus Christ, His last words recorded by John in the Book of Revelation:

"Look! I am coming soon, and my reward is with me to pay each one according to what he has done!" (Rev. 22:12).

Made in the USA
Lexington, KY
18 February 2015